the Venture adventure

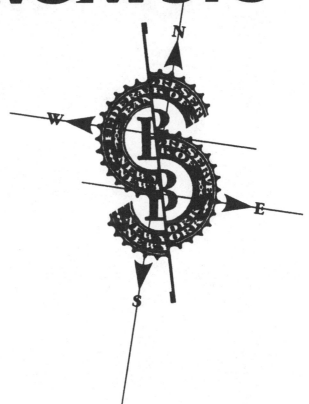

Daryl Bernstein
with Joe Hammond

the Venture adventure

Strategies

for Thriving

in the

Jungle of

Entrepreneurship

BEYOND
WORDS
Publishing
INC

Beyond Words Publishing, Inc.
4443 NE Airport Road
Hillsboro, Oregon 97124-6074
503-693-8700
1-800-284-9673

Design: Principia Graphica
Typography: William H. Brunson Typography Services
Editing: Sue Mann
Proofreading: Marvin Moore

Printed in the United States of America
Distributed to the book trade by Publishers Group West

The corporate mission of Beyond Words Publishing, Inc.:
 Inspire to Integrity

Library of Congress Cataloging-in-Publication Data
Bernstein, Daryl.
    The venture adventure : strategies for thriving in the jungle of
    entrepreneurship / Daryl Bernstein, with Joe Hammond.
        p.   cm.
    Includes bibliographical references.
    ISBN 978-1-885223-09-8   ISBN 1-885223-09-9
    1. New business enterprises.   2. Small business—Management.
    I. Hammond, Joe.   II. Title.
    HD62.5.B483   1996
    658.4′21—dc20   94-44135
                                                                      CIP

For my father, David,

partner in business adventures,

and my mother, Bianca,

mentor in the adventure called life

TABLE of CONTENTS

PART 1

The

Venture

Adventure

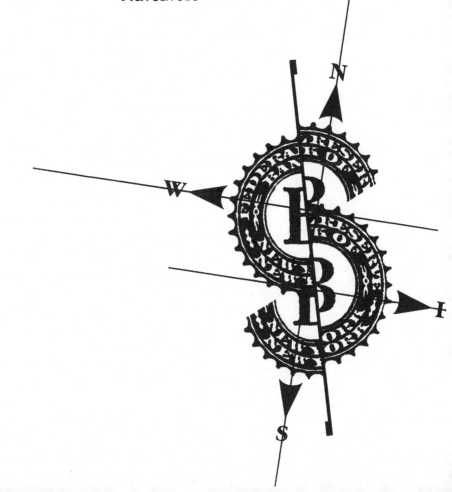

Introduction to Part I

Long ago there lived an incredible old man who had a *magic finger*. He resided alone in the woods, quite a distance from the nearest village. In spite of the distance, however, the old man had garnered quite a reputation among the villagers. You see, his magic finger could turn anything it touched into *solid gold*.

Everyone in the village knew of the old man and visited him quite frequently, bringing objects they wished to be turned into gold. They brought all kinds of things: apples, shoes, books, plates, trinkets—just about anything they could carry—and stood in a typically long line in front of the old man's door. They would often wait for hours just for a touch from the finger of the old man, but of course, the wait was well worth it.

The old man was always very agreeable, no matter how long the lines became. Sometimes he would turn things into gold from dawn till dusk. He greeted each villager with a pleasant smile, happy that he could use his gift to help his fellow citizens. The only thing he asked was that the villagers bring their goods with them: he would not supply the object *and* turn it into gold.

One day a wise young woman from the village, who had heard tales of the man with the magic finger for many years, finally decided to pay him a visit. She trekked through the woods and stood in line quite patiently. Finally, she reached the old man. He looked down at her and noticed that she had not brought anything with her. But being the generous person he was, he decided not to make an issue of it.

The old man picked up a small pebble. He quickly turned it into gold with his magic finger and placed it in her hand. "Here you are, my dear," he said.

But she protested, "Please, just a moment. That's not what I wanted."

"Yes, yes," he replied, not really listening. "I'm very busy today. There are many people waiting. Now you run along home."

The next day, she appeared again. For the second time, she brought nothing with her. The old man, however, did not become the least bit perturbed. He picked up a small twig from the ground, turned it into gold, and handed it to her.

And again she protested. "Please, just a moment. That's not it, that's not it."

But the old man was anxious to serve all the villagers at his door, so he gave her a sincere, friendly smile and sent her home.

Now on the third day she returned once more to the old man's house. This time it was quite early in the morning, and she approached him with ease.

"Well, my dear, I see you've brought nothing with you again. But that's absolutely no problem," he said heartily. He rolled a large log to the doorstep and touched it with his magic finger, turning it into solid gold. "Now, that should keep you satisfied for quite some time, my dear," he said, very pleased with his philanthropy.

"But please, sir," she protested. "That's not it. That's not what I wanted."

"What is it that you *do* want?" he finally asked.

"I want your finger!" she said.

I first heard this story while vacationing on the Greek island of Paros. While I was enjoying lunch on the veranda of a small café, the owner of the establishment introduced himself. The spirited, cheerful old man was quite a conversationalist. As we were discussing the topic of talents, he conveyed this funny, meaningful anecdote.

I have since heard the story several times in slightly different versions. Apparently, the concept of a magic touch is intriguing to people living in many cultures. My café-owner friend, though, derived an interesting lesson from the story. He said, "The message we should take away from this tale is that every person has *at least one magic touch, a special unique talent.* Your talent might be ... how do you say ... ah, to be compassionate. Or maybe to cook. Or to make people happy. But you see, your own magic touch is so special that all the villagers can benefit from it. You have to go out and share it with as many people as you can." Content with his profound instruction, he winked at me and returned to the kitchen.

I wrote this book because I want to give you my magic touch, to teach you the way I approach starting and running small companies. I hope that in sharing with you my perspective on the thrilling world of entrepreneurship, I will give *you* a new magic finger, a skill to turn your dreams not into gold but into reality.

Happiness lies not in the
mere possession of money, it   Franklin D. Roosevelt (1882–1945)
lies in the joy of achievement,   Thirty-second president of the United States
in the thrill of creative effort.

Starting a business is the modern-day equivalent of charging into the jungle in search of lost treasure. And I hope to be your guide—to help you avoid the pitfalls and take advantage of the insights of those who have traveled before you.

Everyone respects adventurers for their courage, innovation, independence, confidence, and self-reliance. People marvel at the risks they assume and the rewards they enjoy. I view modern entrepreneurs as successors to great adventurers. Therefore, throughout this book I relate the stories and insights of prominent explorers, for their wisdom is relevant to the journey of the entrepreneur.

I spend much of my time helping people start and grow businesses. I study phenomenally successful entrepreneurs to discover the strategies they've used to turn good ideas into booming enterprises. I also own and run several companies, which enable me to test the lessons I learn from the masters and develop success strategies of my own. Then I disseminate these entrepreneurial secrets through presentations, seminars, and one-on-one consulting.

At a seminar in London, a well-dressed young man approached me during a break and introduced himself. He ran a large company by day, he said, and assembled a classic-book collection by night. He was interested to know whether I'd read any of the journals by David Livingstone, who explored Africa on behalf of England. I responded with a polite no, ready for the young man to launch into an extended description of the merits of the books. But he said simply, "It's just that your experiences sound quite similar to those of Mr. Livingstone. Well, thank you, anyway." And he walked away.

What could I do? This was too intriguing, so on the way to the airport, I asked the cabbie to stop at a bookshop. I bolted inside, bought a copy of

Missionary Travels and Researches in South Africa by David Livingstone, returned to the cab, and managed to make it to the airport with just a few minutes to spare.

On westward trans-Atlantic flights it is daytime almost the entire way, and I read the book cover to cover. My book-collecting acquaintance was right. I've read practically every book written by entrepreneurs and entrepreneurial thinkers, and not one was as applicable to my businesses as was Livingstone's journal. Ridiculous? Not really. I realized that business isn't only about accounts receivable and price-earnings ratios. Anyone can figure out the technicalities, but *starting and growing your own business is an adventure*. You can reach the treasure only if you set off with the right tools, know the experiences of those who have attempted the expedition before you, and possess the right state of mind for your journey.

I've discovered that the world's most successful entrepreneurs and explorers have much in common. They have the same character traits and use the same strategies to accomplish their missions. Perhaps these success strategies are the keys to phenomenal success in *your* business.

If you're just preparing to start a company, you have a jump on other entrepreneurs. You can apply these strategies from the beginning of your venture. If you currently own a company, you can implement these lessons *now* to increase your profitability and grow your business. The ideas contained in this book work equally well in product-based businesses (pizza shops and bookstores, for example) and service businesses (landscaping companies and consulting firms).

I am an entrepreneur because the entrepreneurial lifestyle is fantastic. It's one challenge after another, one thrill after another, one triumph after another! Every day is invigorating. I wake up at five in the morning because I can't wait to get started attacking the day's challenges. And as a reward for this crazy life, I make a substantial return on my investment. But I don't do it for the money; I do it for the adventure.

You *can* love every day of your life and make a lot of money while you're at it. The secret is in what you're doing and how you're doing it. When you're painting a house, you use your arms and your hands. When you're running a house-painting business, you use a multitude of learned skills: creativity, communication, time management, and organization. That's the beauty of free enterprise: *You use your strengths to make money. You become an entrepreneur by using the resources you have to create wealth*. Robert E. Peary talked of dedicating his "whole being, physical, mental, and moral" to his exploratory pursuits.[1] Apparently his strategy worked, for he discovered the North Pole. To reach *your* North Pole, you, too, must use everything you have.

For the opportunity to enjoy profits, you assume some risk. The fear of risk is the number-one deterrent responsible for preventing people from starting businesses. Of course there's risk! Otherwise, entrepreneurship wouldn't be so exciting. If you're launching a restaurant, you may be gambling your life savings. If you're starting a home-based consulting service, you're gambling your lunch money. Either way, it's a good bet. Why? Because when you buy a lottery ticket, the fate of your investment is out of your hands. You turn on the television at two minutes to ten and watch someone announce the magic numbers. But start a business and you control your destiny. Entrepreneurship is like reaching into the lottery hamper and picking out the numbers *you* want. Sure there's risk, but *you have the power* to generate a high return on your investment!

We hear about phenomenal success stories like Bill Gates of Microsoft and Fred DeLuca of Subway. I've spent plenty of time with millionaires and billionaires, and it's true—they are incredibly talented people. But entrepreneurship isn't just about huge corporations started from scratch. I know a teacher who runs a small home-improvement business. She works on projects each afternoon after she finishes at her school. She is an entrepreneur. An exuberant young man regularly approaches us on the patio of our beach house in Mexico to sell his handmade rugs. He is an entrepreneur. My enthusiastic printer, who employs five people and recently moved into a larger building to accommodate his growth, is also an entrepreneur. Entrepreneurs are defined by *who they are*, not by what they gross.

This book will teach you the rules for successful travel in the jungle of entrepreneurship—how to choose supplies for your journey, assemble your ideal expeditionary team, determine your direction of travel, turn obstacles into advantages, and arrive at your destination with enough energy to enjoy the treasure. As an entrepreneur, you are part of an elite group of courageous people. You have chosen to determine your destiny. You have opted to use your skills for *your* benefit. You have decided to work from five to nine in order not to work from nine to five. Congratulations!

You're in for the adventure of your life.

*The true explorer does his work
not for any hopes of reward or
honour, but because the thing
he has set himself to do is a
part of his being, and must be
accomplished for the sake of
the accomplishment.*

Robert E. Peary (1856–1920)
Discoverer of the North Pole

In any given day, I face a multitude of challenges. My paper supplier
calls and tells me that paper prices are rising—*again*. Our main computer
system crashes. A shipment of products scheduled to arrive yesterday still
doesn't show up. But if I allowed each difficulty to bother me, I'd be a wreck
by the end of the day. Instead, I thrive on difficulties. They make me happy.
They make my day exhilarating.

I believe our spirit is the foundation of our being. By *spirit* I mean perspective—the way we look at the world. Our spirit controls our thoughts,
our actions, and our reactions. It is the most difficult concept in this book to
master and also is the most important.

I see the words *the spirit of entrepreneurship* every time I open a magazine. But this phrase has always bothered me, not so much for what it says
but for the context in which it is used. I read lines like this one: "Americans
want to supplement their incomes, so the spirit of entrepreneurship is once
again flourishing in America." I understand that money is often the primary
motive for starting a business. But if business were just about money, I'd be
doing something else. I do business because business is incredibly exciting.
And the word *entrepreneurship* doesn't adequately convey that excitement,
so I add the word *adventure*. Entrepreneurship is about making money.
Adventure entrepreneurship is about making money and having the time of
your life doing it. Therefore, I will not discuss the spirit of entrepreneurship.
I will discuss *the spirit of adventure entrepreneurship*.

I have accomplished what I have in business because I am brimming
with the spirit of adventure entrepreneurship. I view every event in business as a part of the adventure. Every challenge and every triumph I experience adds to the intensity of my adventure. But it all starts with the
proper spirit. When you learn the spirit, the characteristics and skills will
follow naturally.

When a video store opened near my office, I noted that the business enjoyed all the qualities of a strong retail enterprise—a highly visible storefront location, a large local customer base, and no threatening competitors. Whenever I drove past the store, I noticed several cars parked in the small lot. Several weeks passed and I finally stopped in to rent a video. The store was mobbed, and the cash register was ringing continually. As I was paying, I spoke with the owner, who was working the register. From our one-minute interchange, I realized that he lacked the spirit of adventure entrepreneurship. He had started his company because he "couldn't think of anything else to do." He took little pleasure in the tasks of his business—answering questions about movies, creating displays, and preparing advertisements. And he was quite inflexible—he proudly showed me the sign he had taped to the counter that read VIDEOS *Must* BE BACK ON TIME OR YOU WILL BE CHARGED A $5 PENALTY. Three months later the store was out of business. As far as I could tell, there had been no major changes in his business environment—the area demographics had not changed and no competitors had opened shops nearby. I've seen this situation enough times to know that the most probable cause of failure was lack of spirit.

The lesson is simple—entrepreneurship begins with spirit. And here's the good news: I believe entrepreneurial spirit is learned. We aren't born with it. Reporters ask if I was born an entrepreneur. The answer is no. If I were born an entrepreneur, I would have bartered my mashed bananas for a real meal or would have sold my pacifier to the neighbor's baby. But I didn't. In fact, I didn't show any interest in business until I first turned lemons into lemonade. Sometime between the day I was born and the day I opened my lemonade stand at the age of eight, I picked up the spirit.

Ninety percent of people fascinated by the idea of starting a business never make an effort to act on their ideas. But you have an excellent head start. You're reading this book, so I know you already possess the spirit of entrepreneurship. The question is: Do you have the spirit of adventure entrepreneurship?

Descriptions of entrepreneurship usually include words like *commitment, responsibility*, and *optimism*. These are entrepreneurial *characteristics*, but entrepreneurial *spirit* must come first. To me, spirit is much deeper. Spirit drives behavior. People demonstrate spirit most clearly in their actions, so I will describe the spirit of adventure entrepreneurship by separating it into the following action components. Read on, and absorb the spirit of adventure entrepreneurship.

The Personal Challenge

When asked why he wanted to scale Mount Everest, the English mountain climber George H. L. Mallory replied, "Because it's there."[1] The fact that 29,028 feet of mountain existed between him and the mountaintop was enough to motivate him.

Everyone has felt this impulse, perhaps in less daunting situations, but the impulse is the same nevertheless. You try to open a new jar of mustard, and the lid is on too tight. You *could* eat your sandwich without the mustard, but the jar challenges your determination. So you battle the jar until the lid comes off. Sound familiar?

The same feeling of personal challenge motivates entrepreneurs to start and grow businesses. William Warren complained about the quality of Mexican food in Portland, Oregon. When a friend challenged him to think of something better, he took it personally. He founded Macheezmo Mouse, now a $7 million, twelve-location chain of healthy, fresh, Mexican-food restaurants in the Pacific Northwest.[2]

The Desire for Change

Many entrepreneurs start their businesses out of desperation after losing jobs or arriving from foreign countries. However, most entrepreneurs opt to run businesses not out of need but out of desire. They have experienced the tedium of traditional jobs and want major lifestyle changes, or they want to use their skills and creativity in fulfilling activities. And this involves trading in some security for the opportunity to experience the excitement of entrepreneurial living.

Mungo Park was a young, happily married, established surgeon in Scotland. Dissatisfied with what many would consider a respectable lifestyle, he sought adventure, first on the high seas and then in the perilous jungles of Africa. He ventured across the Senegal Basin, for two months struggling with blistering heat, tropical diseases, irate animals, and even angrier tribal chiefs. At one point, a Muslim chieftain threw him into a filthy jail for four months. But like a true adventurer, he escaped on horseback, made it to the Niger River, and eventually returned to Scotland.[3]

There is nothing wrong with the desire for change. Don't feel guilty about wanting to leave a situation (most commonly a job) for which others would be grateful. The psychologist Abraham Maslow established a hierarchy of needs, a pyramid with physical needs—the most basic—at the bottom and emotional fulfillment at the top.[4] Maslow said that it is natural for human beings to strive for complete fulfillment. Today, perhaps unfortunately, few traditional jobs provide that fulfillment. Fortunately, entrepreneurship does.

If you have kids or know kids, you've heard about the computer game called "Where in the World is Carmen Sandiego?" an interactive, educational global search for fictional criminals. This game, and many other leading educational software programs, comes from the innovative programmers at Brøderbund in San Francisco. This $111 million corporation is the brainchild of Doug Carlston and his brother Gary. And why did Doug Carlston launch Brøderbund? Because he desired a change from the daily routine of his life as a successful lawyer.[5]

The Application of Knowledge

In 1911, when Robert F. Scott set out to become the first person to reach the South Pole, he had some knowledge of the terrain. As a lieutenant in the English Royal Navy, he had spent two years on Ross Island in Antarctica conducting experiments and explorations.[6] In 1985, Gregory Billups left his engineering job in the United States Navy to start Systems, Maintenance & Technology Inc. He used his experience to make it a multi-million-dollar player in the aircraft-services industry. (I won't launch into the technicalities of his business, but *Entrepreneur* magazine said, "SMT's services can be likened to deciding how to design a car to assure efficient, low-cost maintenance.") Billups's former employer now represents 65 percent of his business.[7]

Scott and Billups have something in common. Both used their professional knowledge to become adventurers—Scott on the icy plains of Antarctica and Billups in the perilous jungles of entrepreneurship.

You have some specialized knowledge. Maybe you know food-inventory management from those two months you worked in Mama Mia's Pizzeria, or beer distribution from your year at AAA Beverage Sales, or executive placement from your brief corporate-ladder-climbing stint. Your experiences, even the seemingly insignificant ones, have enriched your knowledge base. And the desire to turn your specialized knowledge into a business venture is a fundamental component of the spirit of adventure entrepreneurship.

A Nonbusiness Goal

Many people start businesses specifically to accomplish a nonbusiness goal—to spend more time with their families, gain more freedom, pay for their children's educations, or support a cause they believe in. Some of the most phenomenal entrepreneurs in the world founded their businesses as a means to fulfill a particular ambition. Their passion for their goals made them exceptionally successful businesspeople.

David Livingstone, perhaps England's most famous explorer, ventured into the challenging African interior with one purpose in mind. By spreading the humanitarian messages of religion, he hoped to stop the flourishing slave trade and alleviate human misery. While pursuing this objective, Livingstone became the first European to cross the African continent and the first to see Victoria Falls (which he named for Queen Victoria), distinguishing himself as an exceptional explorer.[8] He lived the adventure lifestyle while effecting positive social change.

By adopting a nonmonetary goal, you will increase the pleasure you experience running your business. Master entrepreneurs know that money is just the measuring stick of business. Money is not a goal, it is a gauge. Wealth can make you comfortable, but it can't make you happy. An old seasoned New York City cab driver related this wisdom to me: "Ya see, sonny, success is getting what you want, but happiness is wanting what you get." I feel constant joy in knowing I am building a profitable business while improving the lives of others.

Bill Gates, the founder of Microsoft, has a net worth estimated to exceed $10 billion. Forget buying a Ferrari and building a mansion— he could buy the Ferrari company, build a large house for every one of the fifteen thousand Microsoft employees in the world, and still have enough money to fund a lavish lifestyle for the next seven generations of the Gates family. *Surely he isn't working twelve-hour days to earn more money.* Gates exhibits goal-oriented action—he wants to develop cutting-edge technologies, and he uses entrepreneurship as his means.

The Independence Impulse

Jean Jacques Rousseau, the eighteenth-century French philosopher, declared, "Man is born free, yet he is everywhere in chains." A nonconformist all his life, Rousseau believed that human beings as individuals are fundamentally good creatures, and he criticized the constraints government and society place on people's lives.

Most people are like barnacles—they attach themselves to a ship (i.e., a large corporation or government agency) and hang on for the ride. In every generation, though, a few people are individualists who strive for freedom of thought and action. In the mid-1800s, Americans discontented with life in the East streamed westward toward the famed frontier. Today, to exercise this independence, you need not pack your wagon. Instead, pay $12 for a business license and identify yourself as The Jonathan Doodle Company instead of Jonathan Doodle, and you're in business for yourself.

Dependence is limiting. Employees and large organizations have a symbiotic relationship: the workers give their employers a predefined benefit (a specific task) in return for monetary rewards. However, if the workers deviate from their assigned tasks, they may lose their rewards. Also, the organization may undergo changes, forcing the dismissal of workers for no fault of their own. In contrast, as an entrepreneur, you are in control. You act as you wish, and you enjoy—or endure—the consequences of your actions. Because you have no specific, assigned task, you are free to use your creativity and knowledge however you feel they are most productive.

Independence is liberating. Our lives are richer and more exciting when we shape them ourselves rather than when we accept the generic mold imposed on us by our culture. Entrepreneurship is a way for us to express our individuality within the bounds of organized society. The entrepreneur has a desire for independence, the freedom to step to the beat of a different drummer. Thoreau suggested, "Let him step to the music which he hears, however measured or far away." Fortunately, the free-enterprise system allows the entrepreneur to do just that.

Doing the Dream

Jean-Paul Sartre, the founder of a philosophy called "existentialism," believed that people must *act* in order to *be*. He said that everyone has potential, but few ever reach the *action stage* of living. Sartre referred to the *thing-state*, or *être-en-soi*, our state of being while we merely dream about doing something. Prior to action, according to Sartre, we are truly no different from chairs, tables, and other objects in the universe. It is when we act, or become *engagé*, in Sartre's words, that we move from the thing-state to the *person-state*, or *être-pour-soi*. You are truly a person when you act on your dreams.

We've all used the phrases "I could have" and "I would have." You see a successful business and think, "I could have started that." You read a bestseller and think, "I could have written that." Unfortunately, all the *could haves* and *would haves* in the world don't amount to anything. Only action creates results!

At a book signing in Boston, a woman told me she'd driven eighty miles to see me. "Wow," I said. "Thanks for your support."

"Actually," she responded, "I want to tell you about this great business idea I have."

"You drove eighty miles to tell me about a business idea?"

"Yes. It's a very innovative marketing business." And she described what was in fact a great business idea. Working from her home office, she would help local retail businesses market their products nationally, taking a cut of the increased sales resulting from her work.

I asked, "How long did it take you to drive here?"

"Three and a half hours—I got stuck in rush hour."

"Listen," I said, "in the time it took you to drive here, you could have obtained a business license, ordered stationery, written your first advertisement, and still had enough time to go out for a burger. Your idea is excellent, so stop thinking about it. *Do it!*"

When I got back to my office in Arizona, a letter from her was waiting. The postmark indicated that she had mailed it three days after our conversation. She wanted to let me know that in her first two days of work, she had obtained three customers.

Having a great business idea isn't enough. You must do something about it or it will forever rest in the cradle of speculation. There is only one way to discover whether a business idea will produce profit: test it in the marketplace.

A friend of mine in Connecticut is an independent inventor. After spending many years designing products for a major corporation, he decided to pursue a more enriching, entrepreneurial lifestyle. Over a lobster dinner several years ago, he imparted a nugget of wisdom that has remained with me: "When you come up with an idea, someone else in the world has the same idea at the exact same moment. From that point, a race is on—who will be the first person to turn that idea into reality?"

Dreaming and goal-setting are wonderful, but only action produces results. Of course, by taking action, you risk failure. But reflect on the motivating words of Thomas Edison: "People are not remembered by how few times they fail, but by how often they succeed. Every wrong step is another step forward."[9] I believe that every person dreams of an exciting, fulfilling life. Entrepreneurs are the few who *do the dream*.

Your spirit will guide you!

PART II

The Seven

Characteristics

of the Adventure

Entrepreneur

Introduction to Part II

Successful entrepreneurs have a particular personality that differentiates them from other people. Entrepreneurs demonstrate a certain force that powers them toward success. This force, as a whole, is often described as the *entrepreneurial personality*. But this rather daunting phrase implies that you either have it or you don't, that personality is developed over time and that if yours hasn't evolved into the entrepreneurial personality, you may as well throw your business dreams in front of a speeding freight train and resign yourself to a life of burger flipping.

True, there is such a thing as the entrepreneurial mind. However, it is not an immense, mysterious, complex consciousness seeded in the human brain at birth and enhanced during the many stages of growth and development. *The entrepreneurial mind is simply a composite of specific characteristics.*

Through my experience and my contact with many of the world's greatest entrepreneurs, I've discovered that the same characteristics which enabled Columbus to reach the New World also enabled people like Fred Smith, founder of FedEx, to build enormously prosperous companies. Taken together, these characteristics may seem like some ineffable property that differentiates entrepreneurs from others. Separately, however, they aren't so ambiguous. In fact, with a concerted, focused effort, you can learn them rather quickly.

In his book *The Politics*, Aristotle said, "The thing which makes a good man differ from a unit in the crowd is that elements which are elsewhere scattered and separate are here combined in a unity." *Every person has one exemplary characteristic. The great individual, however, has a personality composed of the exemplary characteristics of everyone else.*

As you examine the Seven Characteristics of the Adventure Entrepreneur, you may realize that you already exhibit several of them. You may realize that someone close to you demonstrates one of them exceptionally. But, as Aristotle said, one or two of them makes you just "a unit in the crowd." By mastering all seven, you will acquire the mind-set of the adventure entrepreneur, and you will become extraordinary.

*The only thing
we have to fear
is fear itself.*

Franklin D. Roosevelt (1882–1945)
Thirty-second president of the United States

Courage is a combination of determination, tenacity, and will. It is the characteristic that enables us to confront danger, fear, and other challenges with self-possession and resolution. *Courage is a victory of rational thought over irrational emotion.* Most often, we are hindered from acting not by actual threats to our well-being but by our fear, our emotional response to those threats. *Fear itself is the biggest hindrance to success, and demonstrating courage means defeating emotion with rational judgment.*

Edward Whymper, one of the world's most renowned mountain climbers, had a keen understanding of how mental fortitude can overcome fear. In 1865, this English adventurer became the first human to scale the most imposing of the Swiss Alps, the Matterhorn. The mountain had remained unscaled, according to Whymper, "less on account of the difficulty of doing so, than from the terror inspired by its invincible appearance." The Matterhorn appeared so unconquerable, so intimidating, and so awesome that the local inhabitants had constructed legends around their superstitious fears. Whymper reported that "they spoke of a ruined city on its summit wherein the spirits dwelt . . . and warned one against a rash approach, lest the infuriate demons from their impregnable heights might hurl down vengeance for one's derision."[1]

Though the climb was certainly a daunting physical challenge, the most imposing obstacle faced by potential climbers was *their fear*.

Whymper met this fear with rational deliberation. He attempted on six occasions to scale the mountain but failed each time—mostly because his companions panicked out of fear. Eventually, his determination and perseverance triumphed: five years after first sighting it, he ascended the Matterhorn.

Similarly, most people never attempt the entrepreneurial adventure because they fear failure. It is not the challenges in the jungle of entrepreneurship that stop people from starting businesses. It is the *fear of the challenges in the jungle of entrepreneurship*. The same fear that gripped the Swiss villagers is the apprehension that grips potential entrepreneurs.

Explorers and entrepreneurs encounter two kinds of fear: anticipatory fear (fear of failure) and material fear (fear of losing something tangible—for explorers, their lives; for entrepreneurs, their money).

Anticipatory fear. People are afraid of the mental effects of not reaching a goal. That is, people are afraid of *what they will think of themselves* if they fail. We have a learned association between failure and negative feelings. To avoid negative feelings, we try to avoid situations in which we may not reach our goals. And the easiest way to avoid these feelings is to remain inactive.

Failure is a natural part of your entrepreneurial growth process. Entrepreneurs and explorers alike understand that some degree of failure is common to all adventures. Whymper attempted to scale the Matterhorn six times over a four-year period before finally completing his expedition.

In a speech at the U.S. meeting of the World Economic Forum at Stanford University, Andy Grove, the founder of Intel, said, "You cannot grow a company without continually making mistakes." His words resounded in my head then, and I remember them each time I realize I have erred. *I have learned not to fear making mistakes. Rather, I celebrate mistakes, for they are a sign that I am progressing.*

Potential entrepreneurs often are reluctant to act on their ideas because they are afraid of being ridiculed by family and friends. The fear of being repudiated by others cows us into inaction. But don't look to others for approval. *If your business vision is truly innovative, others will have trouble understanding it.* Ralph Waldo Emerson asked, "But is it so bad then to be misunderstood? Pythagoras was misunderstood, and Socrates . . . and Copernicus, and Galileo, and Newton, and every pure and wise spirit that ever took flesh. To be great is to be misunderstood." Emerson, the great advocate of self-reliance, preached the importance of having courage in the face of opposition.

Increase your courage by focusing on your successes and not on your failures. Baseball players demonstrate this attitude adjustment. If they have a 300 average, they are considered excellent hitters. They're stars even though they have failed 70 percent of the time!

Don't let the fear of failure prevent you from attempting your venture adventure. Failing by refusing to try simply doesn't make sense. It's better to strike out swinging than to strike out looking. In his popular book *A Whack on the Side of the Head*, Roger von Oech suggests, "Differentiate between errors of 'commission' and those of 'omission.' The latter can be more costly than the former. If you're not making many errors, you might ask yourself, 'How many opportunities am I missing by not being more aggressive?'"[2] Errors of commission (mistakes made by committing an error) are more desirable than errors of omission (mistakes caused by not making an effort).

If you don't swing the bat, you'll never learn how to hit a home run. Whymper used the experience he gained from his six failures to help him succeed on the seventh try. And Andy Grove made numerous mistakes in his quest to build Intel into the leading manufacturer of computer chips. If you don't try, you won't be able to learn from your mistakes and try again. Don't look at failure as something to be ashamed of. See failures as growing experiences, lessons that sharpen your entrepreneurial mind.

The fear of failure is the primary cause of inaction. *Mental courage is the ability to stifle your fear of failure and act with confidence.* Acknowledge that a few setbacks will be a natural part of your expedition to reach the top of your Matterhorn, and you can launch your venture adventure with courage.

Material fear. While journeying to the North Pole, Peary and his party persevered through nearly impossible conditions: brutal arctic winds and temperatures that plummeted to nearly 100 degrees below zero Fahrenheit. The biting winds numbed their hands and faces, which sometimes hurt so badly that they could not sleep. But Peary remarked that the best protection against the cold was not warm clothing. "Still the biting cold would have been impossible to face, by anyone not fortified by an inflexible purpose."[3] Courage in the face of material fear enabled Peary to reach the northernmost point on planet Earth.

For explorers, physical courage is bravery in the face of serious threats to their personal safety. For entrepreneurs, physical courage is fortitude in risking material goods—most often money. Maria Barraza used her $50,000 life savings to launch Barraza Associates Ltd., a private-label clothing-design company. She had the courage to face the possibility of financial ruin. And her courage paid off. In her first year of business, she generated more than $100,000 in sales—more than double her startup costs. Several years later, her annual sales exceeded $2 million.[4]

Entrepreneurship requires courage to overcome material fear. You must be willing to risk some of your assets. Risk as little as possible, but you will have to risk something when you launch your venture adventure. *Business is a combination of speculation and compensation, and success is simply the desired ratio between the two.*

My favorite children's book is Maurice Sendak's *There's a Nightmare in My Closet.*⁵ It's the story of a boy who's afraid to go to sleep at night because he thinks there is a terrible monster living in his closet.

Finally, the boy becomes fed up. He takes his cork gun, opens the closet door, and shoves the monster into the room. When he turns on the lights and looks at the monster, he realizes how silly he was to be afraid. The monster isn't scary at all; in fact, he's rather cute. The boy and the monster turn out to be terrific pals. The nightmare crawls into bed with the boy, and they have a slumber party.

The boy overcomes his fear by leading his nightmare out of the closet and into his room where he can see it. After the boy confronts his fear and learns to understand it, he's no longer afraid. *Rational thought triumphs over emotion.*

Fear is an irrational, emotional response to things we don't understand. We all have a giant, enigmatic, obscure fear. We never stop to define this fear, to analyze its components. Our fear is like the nightmare in the closet. In our heads it is big, looming, and threatening, but in reality it is just the aggregate of a variety of small, simple apprehensions.

Flush your fear out of the closet and look it straight in the eye. You will find that your fear of business is a combination of several specific worries. Perhaps you're afraid of losing a portion of your savings, giving up your comfortable job with its steady income, or being ridiculed by friends who believe your business idea is foolish.

Identify the exact components of your overall fear. Examine them rationally one at a time. You'll realize that many of them are unsubstantiated. For example, if you're afraid of losing your initial investment, realistically evaluate the risks involved. If you're apprehensive about giving up your job to pursue an entrepreneurial adventure, rationally assess the benefits and detriments of both your job and the entrepreneurial lifestyle.

Your best weapon against fear is clear, logical, sensible thinking. Having the courage to face your fear, your monstrous nightmare in the closet, is little more than getting to know it a little better. In the jungle of entrepreneurship, fear itself is the only real obstacle. When you take the time to examine your fear, you'll find that there really isn't anything to be afraid of.

Pull your fear out of the closet and look it in the eye.

| CHAPTER | 4 | Optimism |

*What if there is a
third factor—optimism
or pessimism—that matters
as much as talent or desire?*

Martin E. P. Seligman
Psychology professor and author

The optimist is the person who walks into a restaurant planning to pay for her oyster dinner with the pearl she will find inside it. We've all heard optimist jokes. They're funny, but unlike other kinds of jokes, they're often representative of reality. Optimism is indeed laughable; optimists seem to be anachronistic to our complex modern society.

Optimism versus Pessimism

As human beings we all have a special lens—a developed brain— through which we see the world. We all use our lenses a little bit differently. Those of us who are optimistic choose to focus our lenses on the flowers, the trees, the beauty around us. Others choose to focus their lenses on the weeds. But optimism is a serious issue, because *optimism influences achievement*.

Discussing the relationship between optimism and entrepreneurship in his book *Mid-Career Entrepreneur*, Joseph Mancuso says that we can tell if people are entrepreneurs by examining the way they start their cars. The entrepreneur gets in the car, starts the engine, and drives off, adjusting the seat, radio, air conditioning, mirrors, and seat belt as the car approaches the speed limit. Other people, who Mancuso calls the hired hands, make all these adjustments, make themselves comfortable, and then start the car.

The ultimate test, says Mancuso, is when the entrepreneur is the passenger. As the hired hand adjusts the seat, radio, air conditioning, mirrors, and seat belt, the entrepreneur shouts, "For goodness sake, start the car!"[1]

Entrepreneurs don't worry about potential problems down the road. They are anxious to get started, so they just get in their cars and drive. *Successful entrepreneurs are optimists. They expect the best possible outcome, and they dwell on the most hopeful aspects of every situation.*

A shoe merchant sent his sons to a remote country to investigate the shoe market. The first son wrote, "Dad, the natives here don't wear shoes. There's no market. I'm coming home." The other son wrote, "Dad, the natives don't wear shoes. I've never seen such a big opportunity. Send over a ship full of shoes!" Both sons examined *the same situation*. One chose to dwell on the negative aspects. The other saw only the positive.

Master entrepreneurs put themselves in an optimistic frame of mind to prevent negativity from hampering their momentum. Marc Ham and Carol Bieber co-founded Flapdoodles Inc., a Newark-based children's clothing company, in 1982. Ham, a former clothing-store manager, and Bieber, a teacher, didn't have much experience in entrepreneurship when they launched their venture adventure, and they faced a huge competitive challenge in taking on the major labels.

They had one major strength—a good idea for all-cotton kids wear, what *Entrepreneur* magazine called "bright mix-and-match coordinates."[2] But I believe they had one other incredible asset: their optimism. They could have thought about all the negative aspects of their venture into the competitive clothing business, like their lack of experience, manufacturing facility, and distribution system. Instead, Ham and Bieber chose to focus on the positive. Ten years after its launch, Flapdoodles boasted a 67,000-square-foot factory and sales topping $20 million.

Thor Heyerdahl, one of this century's most optimistic adventurers, set out in 1947 to prove that Polynesia was originally populated by South Americans, not by Asians as most anthropologists had theorized. He sought to prove his point by demonstrating the migratory process used by ancient South Americans. He launched a primitive raft, which he called the *Kon Tiki*, from the Peruvian coast, intending to let the natural ocean current carry him to Polynesia.

Most people believed Heyerdahl to be embarking on a suicide mission, and they had plenty of reason to doubt his sanity. The balsa wood of the raft was so porous and fragile that it would likely break apart in the ocean swells or become waterlogged and sink. With only a bamboo hut as shelter, *Kon Tiki* expedition members would be at the mercy of the waves and the weather. The ropes that bound the wood together would break under the strain of grinding logs. And even if the *Kon Tiki* managed to stay afloat, it could never navigate the deep, rough ocean swells.

Heyerdahl, though, refused to waver in his optimism. He set sail amid the negative cries of his many doubters, and 101 days and 4,300 miles later, the entire crew of the *Kon Tiki* arrived on a small Polynesian island healthy and intact.[3] Heyerdahl was aware of the negative aspects of his journey, and

I suspect he was a little frightened by the prospect of losing his life during the course of his adventure. *But he chose to focus only on the positive aspects of his expedition; he didn't allow his negative thoughts to prevent him from attempting the journey.*

Although Heyerdahl chose to ignore the negative aspects of his ambitious expedition, sometimes it's better not to be aware of them at all. Livingstone focused so intently on his adventure that he didn't think about the adverse and hostile forces surrounding him in the jungle. On one occasion, he waded near the shore of a river looking for materials with which to build a raft. "I worked many hours in the water," he remembered, "for I was not then aware of the number of alligators in the Zouga, and never think of my labours without feeling thankful that I escaped their jaws."[4] I don't mean to advise you to wade in alligator-infested rivers, but the lesson of the story is applicable to business: *Don't waste energy worrying about what may go wrong. If something will go wrong, it will go wrong, and you'll deal with it when it happens. Instead, expend your energy building an enjoyable, fulfilling, and rewarding business.*

Every circumstance in life and in business has both negative and positive aspects. Eating an ice-cream cone has negative and positive aspects. Taking a taxi has negative and positive aspects. Sitting has negative and positive aspects. Getting married has negative and positive aspects. Moving to another city has negative and positive aspects. You can focus on the bad aspects or the good. It's up to you.

Here's an example. The Saudi Arabian government, in an effort to protect its workers from the intense Middle Eastern sun, places orders with two small sunglasses manufacturers in Phoenix: Four Eyes Inc. and FrameCo. Both companies receive the same order—ten thousand pairs of black-framed sunglasses with mirrored lenses.

The founder and CEO of Four Eyes, Ceda Light, is elated! She runs home and tells her husband, "This is the biggest order Four Eyes has ever received! This order alone will generate $40,000 in profit! Serving the Saudi Arabian government is going to give us fantastic international publicity! This could be the start of something big! Maybe Iran and Libya will follow suit and buy glasses from us, too!" Elizabeth and her husband break out the champagne to celebrate.

U. V. Rays, owner of FrameCo, has a different perspective. He goes home to his wife and announces, "I'm in for some long, sixteen-hour days for the next month. No relaxing for me. And I'll have to buy more machinery to handle the increased output. That's going to drain my cash reserves. And I don't even want to begin to think about how the hell I'm going to ship a

Mack truck full of sunglasses from Phoenix to Riyadh." A fantastic opportunity walks in his front door, and Mr. Rays can't think of anything but the inconveniences this big order will cause him.

Both Ms. Light and Mr. Rays are in the same situation, but each entrepreneur sees it very differently. In the long run, Four Eyes Inc. will thrive and FrameCo probably won't. But, more important, Ceda Light will enjoy running her business and U. V. Rays will be miserable.

Increase Your Optimism

Visualize success. If you have a difficult time looking at the positive aspects of life, *increase your level of optimism by using your imagination to visualize success.* Set aside a few minutes each day to perform some mental exercises. Sit back on the couch or lie on your bed, close your eyes, and open your imagination. Picture yourself receiving a large order, ringing up huge receipts, or making a tough sell. Imagine yourself smiling and feeling good; imagine the expressions of your family and friends when they hear the good news. Visualize good things happening to you, and you'll learn to expect the best possible outcome from your adventure. Your visions gradually will become real.

Exercise. I've found that certain activities increase my optimism and make me feel positive. I like to start off every day with a jog. And it doesn't have to be a marathon—just a short run to get my blood flowing and some air in my lungs. Exercises like running, walking, swimming, and bike riding, which tend to be a little monotonous, are very meditative and can be mentally therapeutic. *Exercise releases certain chemicals in the brain that promote positive thinking.* Exercise produces a natural high.

Listen to music. Listening to upbeat music can help change my moods. Occasionally, I jump into my car and take a short drive to a nice, isolated spot with a beautiful view of the desert. Then I pop in a CD and rejuvenate myself. Music has a special, almost magical, ability to change your frame of mind. *Listening to upbeat music can instantly put you in a positive mood.*

Stick to the facts. Perhaps the most pragmatic way to become more optimistic is to systematically defeat your negative thoughts by factually disproving them. For many people, thinking positive thoughts won't do the trick. Martin E. P. Seligman notes in his groundbreaking book *Learned Optimism*, "Merely repeating positive statements to yourself does not raise mood or achievement."[5] *Instead of trying to force yourself to accept happy thoughts, focus on rationally disproving negative thoughts.*

If you were U. V. Rays, for example, you could easily disprove your negative thoughts by doing a little homework. You could read a good time-management book, like Stephen Covey's *First Things First*,[6] and discover that producing ten thousand pairs of sunglasses in a month shouldn't require you to expend any more energy than you would producing one thousand pairs. Call a shipping broker, and you would find that shipping a product to Saudi Arabia isn't much more difficult than shipping it across state lines. By examining your negative thoughts closely, you'll be able to squelch your pessimism with optimism.

Perspective is a function of how we deal with problems. People who maintain a positive perspective generally externalize their problems. People with chronically pessimistic attitudes tend to internalize problems—they blame themselves for causing their predicaments. "The optimists," in the words of Seligman, "believe that defeat is not their fault: circumstances, bad luck, or other people brought it about. Such people are unfazed by defeat. Confronted by a bad situation, they perceive it as a challenge and try harder." Optimism is the difference between viewing your obstacles as challenges and viewing them as irritating hindrances.

According to Shakespeare, "Every cloud engenders not a storm." There are many clouds in the jungle of entrepreneurship. The happy, prosperous adventure entrepreneur admires the beauty of the cirrus, cumulus, nimbus, and stratus formations. When rain blankets the land, the adventure entrepreneur finds cover and appreciates the power of nature. The pessimistic explorer, however, suffers in the jungle of entrepreneurship and cowers in fear that all the clouds will bring rain. The pessimistic explorer never leads an expedition across the plains for fear of being caught in the open when rain falls. Both adventurers are traveling in the same jungle. Each sees it from a different perspective.

Focus your lens on the flowers, not on the neighboring weeds.

*Change is the
very essence of life.* Anatole France (1844–1924)
French novelist

Aesop's fable "The Oak and the Reed" conveys a vivid lesson on flexibility. The massive Oak, proud of its height and its strength, looked upon the smaller, thinner Reed with a bit of pity. The Oak remarked about how frustrating it must be to bend under the weight of birds, to which the small but wise Reed replied, "You, and not I, should pay the winds respect. I bow, but do not break."

Soon, a vicious northerly wind burst forth from the horizon and swept through the forest with furious speed. It whipped through the trees and shrubs with unremitting power. The force of the gale was so mighty that the Oak began to tremble under the stress, until finally it broke at the trunk. The Reed, however, bent easily under the force of the wind; its thin, durable structure allowed it to weather the storm.

Inflexibility is misinterpreted as strength, when it is, in fact, a weakness. *Strong businesses and strong entrepreneurs share the characteristics of the reed: the ability to bend without breaking.* In the jungle of entrepreneurship, where constant change is the norm, only flexible adventurers will be able to survive and thrive.

Flexibility for Success

Successful entrepreneurs are aware of possible change and are willing to adapt to it. Jim Johnson, founder and owner of Hi-Country Beef Jerky, has proven the value of flexibility in his twenty years in business. This Montana-based entrepreneur got his start when local hunters stopped by his grocery store and asked him to smoke and marinate their meats. Johnson's jerky was savory and delicious. Hi-Country Beef Jerky became quite popular, and within a few years Johnson distributed his product throughout the surrounding states and Canada.

The quality of Johnson's jerky brought him initial success, but flexibility allowed him to maintain solid growth. Located in Lincoln, just ten miles west of the Continental Divide, Hi-Country Beef Jerky regularly faces the challenge of inclement mountain weather, which often causes problems for local distribution. Recently, unusual weather conditions stretched the snowfall into May, hampering distribution to outlet stores in surrounding states by 40 percent. At the same time, an influx of jerky products from South America heightened the competition within the larger U.S. market.[1]

Johnson responded by bending his business in another direction. "I focused my efforts on the business's smallest division, the local market," Johnson explained to me. Realizing that his jerky-distribution business was becoming increasingly difficult, he diversified by opening a new retail outlet in his area. The store, a refurbished museum decorated with local artifacts and a slew of Johnson's hunting trophies, features products from all over Montana. Nearly three hundred businesses—most owned by small-time entrepreneurs who otherwise might not have an opportunity to display their products—share the shelf space. Customers will find everything from arts and crafts to handmade knives to local food products, including Johnson's beef jerky.

When I asked Johnson how his flexibility will affect his business, he responded, "Not only will my volume of business triple within the year, I expect profits to triple as well." In spite of competition from South American jerky producers and constant fluctuation in the Rocky Mountain weather, *Johnson has kept his business profitable for nearly two decades because he has remained flexible.*

Adventure entrepreneurship is an unpredictable lifestyle. Your goals will include making money and enjoying the experience, and in pursuit of these goals you will stray far off the traveled path. Johnson's transition from distributor to retailer is not unusual. *The jungle of entrepreneurship will challenge you constantly. You will have to undergo regular change to survive and thrive.* Don't be surprised if you start out selling bagels and end up manufacturing underwear.

Ardis Gant and Jack Ralph, co-owners of Law Enforcement Equipment Company, have created a successful business by expecting change at the most unexpected times. This Kansas City, Missouri, company supplies police departments and other government agencies with firearms, bulletproof vests, handcuffs, car sirens, and other handy utensils.

The partners have pushed sales to more than $6.5 million by being very flexible. In an interview with *Entrepreneur* magazine, Gant conveyed one customer's request: "The Nebraska Highway Patrol called us one night at ten o'clock and said, 'Bring all the tear gas you have.'" Understanding the value of the flexibility trait, Gant and Ralph "loaded up a car and met them in Omaha at three in the morning."[2] Sending a delivery truck first thing in the morning wouldn't have been enough. Their customer had an immediate need, and they filled it—even in the middle of the night.

Tom Novotny and Todd Revesz, co-owners of Chicago's Planet Cafe, are not just receptive to change, they *thrive* on it. When it became too difficult to control tardiness—they couldn't get their employees into the cafe early in the morning—Novotny and Revesz came up with a great idea: they would allow employees to come to work in their pajamas! The customers enjoyed the employees' scruffy, just-got-out-of-bed-and-I'm-still-half-asleep look so much that they now come to Planet Cafe dressed in their pajamas, too![3]

Open minds and relaxed attitudes have taken the owners of Planet Cafe on the adventure ride of their lives. By being open to change and receptive to new ideas—the hallmarks of enthusiastic learners—Novotny and Revesz have kept their business on the cutting edge and have gained national recognition for their innovation.

To guide your expedition to the treasure, you must be flexible. *Flexibility in the face of unexpected and unwanted change enables explorers to complete a successful journey*. In business, there are two kinds of flexibility: planned and reactive. Gant and Ralph demonstrate planned flexibility—they plan to do whatever is necessary to serve their customers. Therefore, when the Nebraska Highway Patrol needed tear gas immediately, the two entrepreneurs drove to Omaha in the middle of the night. Reactive flexibility is the act of changing under force. Johnson practiced reactive flexibility when he diversified his business to meet mounting challenges in the beef-jerky industry.

Inflexibility Means Failure

Inflexibility results in lost business. In France I encountered entrepreneurs who gave new meaning to the word *inflexible*. One evening in Paris, we were strolling along the Seine and, not in the mood for a full dinner, wandered into a patisserie in search of some pastries. The time was 6:05—five minutes after the shop's posted closing time. From the outside I saw a robust woman cleaning up behind the counter, and I noticed that the display case was still fairly full of pastries. The French patisserie chefs don't use preservatives, so they have to throw out all unsold baked goods at the end of the day. I was sure the woman would be rather pleased to sell more pastries before closing the shop.

But as I wandered into the shop, the woman, with a sudden look of anger on her face, came barreling out from behind the counter, waving rolling pin in the air, yelling, *"Vous ne pouvez pas lire le panneau? Le magasin est fermé!"* ("Can't you read the sign? The store is closed!")

Needless to say, I try to avoid angry French women armed with rolling pins, so I ran out. I was stunned! I had walked into the store five minutes after closing and had been chased away. And the display case was filled with food! She could have made an easy sale, and I probably would have returned to her patisserie several more times because my hotel was nearby. I couldn't help but gape at her lack of flexibility.

Several months later, after a long session, ten friends and I wandered out of a hotel in Chicago in search of food. We were all quite hungry, and we stopped at the first restaurant we found, a rather expensive trattoria. Ten hungry diners wandering in on a slow Wednesday evening is a lucky break for this restaurateur, I was thinking, when the owner emerged from the kitchen. He looked at us, promptly proclaimed, "My restaurant will not open for ten more minutes," and walked back into the kitchen. Amazed, we walked out, and the restaurateur lost several hundred dollars worth of business.

Many qualities of the adventure entrepreneur are secondary to flexibility. Strength, courage, and determination are important qualities for success in any profession, but entrepreneurship is unique. You must take care not to allow strength to overwhelm flexibility—remember what happened to IBM in the 1980s. Use your flexibility to meet change. Your ability to adapt to transformations in the marketplace will enable your business to continue to grow even under the most trying circumstances.

In *Awaken the Giant Within*, Anthony Robbins writes, "There will be times when there are things you will not be able to control, and your ability to be flexible in your rules, the meaning you attach to things, and your actions will determine your long-term success or failure, not to mention your level of personal joy."[4]

Strive to be a reed, not an oak.

We don't see things as they are, we see them as we are.

Anaïs Nin (1903–1977)
French-born American writer

Thomas J. Watson Sr., the founder of IBM, had a mysterious sense of confidence in his business and in himself. One wintery evening in 1924, Watson came home and proudly proclaimed that his company, the Computing-Tabulating-Recording Company, would henceforth be known as International Business Machines. His family stood with mouths agape, wondering at his audacity. International Business Machines was quite an illustrious name for a small company that sold coffee grinders, butcher scales, Oriental rugs, and a few cash registers in New York City.

His family thought the name was ludicrous. His son, Thomas J. Watson Jr., in his book *Father, Son and Co.*, recalls, "I guess Dad thought linking Oriental rugs and meat scales was splendid, but I found it embarrassing."[1] The business was not international, and it had very little to do with business machines. *However, the senior Watson had a vision of where he wanted to take his business, and he had the self-confidence necessary to turn his vision into reality.*

Self-Confidence

Adventure entrepreneurs are marked by an intense degree of self-confidence. They have a curious ability to maintain belief in themselves and their ideas, even when their visions seem preposterous to the rest of the world. This strong belief, this self-confidence, is the impetus for success and is the driving force behind adventure entrepreneurs. Without complete reliance on their ideas and total confidence in their visions of the future, their survival in the jungle would be nearly impossible.

Unwavering belief in their ideas and the ability to realize their dreams are characteristics shared by modern-day entrepreneurs and master explorers alike. Livingstone ignored widely accepted geographical theories when he decided to explore the most remote regions of Africa. Europe's finest geographers and cartographers believed Africa to be a vast sandy desert, devoid of resources necessary to sustain human life. However, Livingstone, our heroic adventurer, believed Africa to be remarkably fertile. He wrote, "My deliberate conviction was and is, that the part of the country indicated is as capable of supporting millions of inhabitants as it is of its thousands."[2] He never wavered in his belief, and his discoveries proved the geographers' theories incorrect. Livingstone's confidence in himself was a purposeful, intentional, and conscious effort; it was a deliberate act of his will to believe in his ideas.

Livingstone was of such character that he used the doubts of others to motivate himself, to strengthen his faith. When people thought him incapable of something, when others doubted his ability, he became more self-confident. Early in his travels, Livingstone's native guides doubted his ability to make the rugged journey through the jungle because of his slender appearance. He wrote, "This made my Highland blood rise, and I kept them all at the top of their speed for days together, until I heard them express a favourable opinion of my pedestrian powers."[3] *His guides' doubts about his ability did not discourage him. Rather, he harnessed this skepticism and used it as a mental propulsion, a motivating force.*

Entrepreneurs also possess this sense of self-confidence, this fiery belief in themselves. Steven Jobs and Steven Wozniak, displaying a brash but controlled degree of faith in their idea, proceeded with their plan to build an accessible, unintimidating personal-computer system even though Hewlett-Packard and Atari (their employers at the time) rejected their plan. Undaunted, the duo founded Apple Computer.[4]

I promise you that your business adventure will take you places you can't dream of right now. No matter what kind of business you run, at some point you will find yourself blazing a trail through the wilderness, heading into uncharted territory. Peary described the pioneering spirit he and his crew felt as they searched for the North Pole: "We are beyond the world's highways now, and shall see no sail or smoke except our own, until we return."[5] *Your venture adventure will take you off the paved road of traditional employment and into the rugged jungle of entrepreneurship.* Most people around you will opt to stay on the paved road. You must have a strong belief in yourself, your ideas, and your business to survive and thrive in your trailblazing journey.

In their book *The Confidence Quotient*, Meryle Gellman and Diane Gage relate what Marcus Allen, a trophy winner and football great, said: "You have to believe in yourself. The other day I looked in the mirror and said, 'Boy, you look good.' A friend teased me about being vain, but I smiled and said, 'If nobody else is going to tell me I look good, I'm gonna tell myself.' I don't consider myself vain, I just want to keep striving to be the best I can be."[6] Allen simply *believes* in himself; others are free to interpret his behavior as they please. He realizes that his vision of himself affects his performance.

Boost Your Self-Confidence

Your vision of yourself is important because the self-image you construct creates a self-fulfilling prophecy. If you are confident and believe good things will happen to you, you'll be more likely to create a lifestyle that will fulfill that vision. However, if you have a low level of self-confidence, if you believe problems will hinder your life experience, then you'll be more likely to fashion a lifestyle that fulfills such a prophecy. We have a tendency to validate our opinions of ourselves.

Fortunately, self-confidence is a learned characteristic. It is not a genetically inherited trait only of people fated to become successful. Some people are incredibly confident in themselves, not because they are smarter, more attractive, or more experienced than others, but because *they have learned this behavior*. Most often, self-confidence is a result of strong parenting. In *The Confidence Quotient*, Allen says, "I have very few self-doubts because my parents gave me a great foundation of love and emotional support. They taught me it's important to dream and to work hard to make my dreams materialize."[7]

Those of us who were lucky enough to have supportive, encouraging parents have a head start. However, life experiences such as school, employment, and relationships often damage self-confidence. Everyone can use a boost in self-confidence. The following three-step process can help you strengthen your belief so you can charge through the jungle of entrepreneurship free from the inhibitions of self-doubt.

Unravel the source of your disbelief. Your attitudes about yourself were formed in your earlier years. By the time you were four or five years old, the foundation of your personality had been laid. From the moment of your birth, people in your life—parents, siblings, peers, teachers—crafted your self-image by how they interacted with you.

Think back to your childhood and ask yourself how your parents and other influential people in your life treated you. Identify people whose comments and criticisms may have suppressed your self-confidence. This task requires a high level of introspection and thoughtfulness, but it is the key to dispelling the negative attitudes you have about yourself.

Situations and experiences also may have influenced your degree of belief in yourself. A particularly bad Little League season or a ruthless history class may have diminished your faith in your ability. I won't lead you on a journey into your psyche in search of influential experiences; this is best left to a psychodynamic therapist. However, I want you to determine which people and experiences may have caused your lack of belief, because in the next step we will examine those causes.

Analyze and dispel your disbeliefs. Disbelief is often a singular, looming force in our heads. Disbelief, though, is just a combination of all the comments, criticisms, and experiences you identified in step one. If you allow these negative influences to stay lumped together in your mind, your disbelief will overpower your motivation and you will remain inactive. However, after you've identified the sources of your negative self-image, you can deal with them one at a time. Separate them in your mind. Perhaps listing them on paper will help you to visualize each influence as a single unit.

Now, proceed through the list systematically and evaluate each item. Think about it logically and rationally. By examining each influence, you will realize how senseless your self-doubts are. For example, perhaps one of your negative influences is "Parents punished me for getting a C in fifth grade." You remember that your parents derided you for getting a C in math, even though all your other grades were A's and B's. By isolating and examining this incident, you can think logically and rationally: you can be proud of your report cards—the A's and B's overshadowed one shortcoming.

Systematically evaluating your early interactions and experiences allows you to disqualify the causes of your self-doubt. You can eliminate your inhibiting forces and put faith in your ability.

Recognize the power of your ideas. Too often we look to others to approve our ideas. We base our opinions of ourselves on other people's opinions of us and our ideas. Many potential entrepreneurs have never launched expeditions because friends, family members, and industry professionals have criticized their business concepts. All that should concern you is what *you* think, believe, and envision. Pay no attention to the judgments of others. Have faith in your ideas, because you know the power of your mind.

The ability to create personal happiness is a power you alone possess. With a steady belief in your vision of your business, your lifestyle, and your future, you have a greater chance of turning your dreams into reality. And self-confidence is the foundation of entrepreneurial success, not just in the startup stage but in the day-to-day operation of the business as well. Cultivate the characteristic of belief in yourself. Nurture it through self-reflection. Strengthen it by focusing on your achievements.

The most successful entrepreneurs of our time have found treasure where others believed none existed. Adventure entrepreneurship is about determining the approximate location of a treasure and launching an expedition to reach it. You can be sure the treasure actually exists only when you've reached it, so during your journey your belief in its existence must keep you going.

Whether you believe you can or you believe you can't, you're right.

Wherever you see a successful business, someone once made a courageous decision.

Peter Drucker (b. 1909)
American business philosopher and author

In the enchanting hills outside Florence, Italy, I found the ultimate symbol of indecisiveness. We vacationed in a beautiful villa in San Donato, a small community overlooking Florence. At one point, the road from Florence into the hills branches into several directions. A classic European signpost on a cement block is in the middle of the road. Four signs adorn the post, each announcing the direction of a town in the hills: Bigallo straight ahead, Arezzo to the left, and San Donato and Incisa to the right.

Here's the hilarious part of the story. The sign has been mangled by indecisive motorists who have run into it because they couldn't make up their minds where they wanted to go. *They simply couldn't decide quickly enough which direction to turn, so they smashed right into the sign.*

"Think long, think wrong" is how the kids at school used to explain it when we played gin rummy. Should you pick a card from the top of the deck or go for the discard pile? Such choices can be pretty important when you're nine years old and your reputation hinges on a card game. Even in third grade, indecisiveness was a losing characteristic!

I knew I would be beginning this chapter today (a Saturday), so yesterday at my office I counted all the decisions I had made over the course of the day. My final count was forty-three. Just to give you an idea, in the hour between eleven and twelve o'clock I had to decide whether to

- Take a call from the president of a new computer company in town or ask my receptionist to say I was busy
- Approve the purchase of new overhead lights for the production area or request another solution for the lighting problem
- Make full payment on a large invoice from our paper supplier or maintain an account payable until next month

- Have lunch at my desk or go out
- Hire temporary workers to handle the week's increased volume or make do with our staff

If I had taken very long to reach a decision on each of yesterday's issues, today I would still be at my desk working on yesterday's business!

Making the Right Choice

Indecisiveness has always been a serious problem for the world's great explorers. Imagine you're trekking through the frozen arctic terrain, a bitter wind cutting against your neck. All of a sudden, you turn to your right and see a flesh-eating polar bear charging at you! With your unloaded flintlock rifle stashed in your sled, you don't have much time to decide what to do.

Can you imagine the trouble Livingstone would have been in if he had stopped to consider all his options while one hundred agitated natives with bows drawn and spears at the ready charged him? The jungle of entrepreneurship won't afford you much time to make decisions, either. You must be prepared to make quick, clear, definitive choices.

Identifying all the possible options in a situation and giving rational, deliberate thought to each is a good decision-making process. The problem, however, is that many people cannot stop deliberating. They continue to weigh the options and consider the possibilities until it's too late: they smash right into the road sign!

Many people put off decision making because they fear making the wrong choice. They aren't pleased by the likely consequences of any option and thus are hesitant to choose. Others are uncertain of the possible outcomes and are restrained from making a decision. They worry about what may happen if they make the wrong decision.

What most people fail to realize, though, is that the success of any decision is not dependent on choosing the "correct" option. Instead, the success of a decision depends on your ability to *make your choice the right choice*. Whichever option you choose will be the right one if you make it right. *Decisiveness is a function of your ability to choose an option quickly and then devote yourself to effecting the results you want from it.*

Making the Choice Right

Each time you're faced with a decision, remember that each possibility has advantages and disadvantages. Selecting an option means accepting its strengths and weaknesses and giving up the strengths and weaknesses of the other options. You must accept the reality that you cannot receive the benefits of all the options—in life, you cannot have your cake and eat it, too. You will have to give up the benefits of the other options to enjoy the benefits of the option you select.

You can use several strategies to become more decisive.

Follow what I call the "One-Day Rule." *Cut down on time spent deliberating over a problem.* Allow an item requiring a decision to rest on your desk for only one day. If it lounges around for longer than a day, it hurts your productivity. When a proposal or a sales letter crosses my desk, I hold it in my hands only once. I may spend some time reading it and evaluating it, but when I put it down I have made my decision. I don't read it, then put it down, then pick it up later and read it again, and so on. As a result, my in-pile never grows taller than my out-pile.

Use metaphors to help put your decisions in perspective. *By placing your problems within a metaphorical context, you can create new ways of looking at your challenges.* This book uses a metaphor to make the rather daunting entrepreneurial process more understandable, vivid, and exciting. Thinking of yourself as an adventurer guiding an expedition through the jungle provides you with a different perspective on the entrepreneurial process.

Know what your priorities are. Only then can you make decisions that will help you fulfill them. Your decision-making process will be easier when you've determined a general idea of where you want to be in life. Later in the book, I'll help you construct a vision of your ideal lifestyle. With this vision in mind, you'll be able to quickly eliminate several options in a given situation that obviously will not help you reach your vision.

Select an option and commit yourself wholeheartedly to it. Dedicate yourself to extracting from it the ends you desire. Devote 100 percent of your energy toward effecting the results you want. *Direct all your emotional, mental, and physical energy toward making that option work for you.* The writer Emory S. Adams Jr. says, "When a decision has been made and the die is cast, then murder the alternatives."[1] These words capture the aggressive determination necessary to master the decisiveness trait. Approach the decision-making process as if you intend to take no prisoners. Seize an option and make it the *right* option.

Don't second-guess yourself. *If you begin to reconsider discarded options, you take valuable energy away from the task at hand.* If you're thinking about the options you chose not to select, you're not putting all your energy into the decision you did select. Commit yourself to the decision you made and do everything within your power to make it the *right* decision.

Selecting an option isn't the same as making a decision. Selecting an option means discarding the other alternatives, but you haven't made a decision until you take a positive action toward making your option the right one. Perhaps the Italian motorists had decided which direction they wanted to turn, but they hadn't taken the positive action necessary to turn their decision into reality.

A decision is like a fork in the road;
it forces you to take responsibility for the
direction of your journey.

Why not seize the pleasure at once? How often is happiness destroyed by preparation, foolish preparation?

Jane Austen (1775–1817)
English novelist

Thought creates ideas, but only action creates results. You can use your creativity, courage, and belief to create and develop an idea for a workable business, but that idea will remain theoretical, merely a conceptual speculation, unless you take active steps to bring it to life. The jungle of entrepreneurship does not afford you much time to think, evaluate, or theorize. You must act *fast*, not just on your business ideas but also on the day-to-day challenges of guiding an entrepreneurial expedition. Adventure entrepreneurs are smart, thoughtful, and deliberate, but they are confident in taking immediate action.

Think how many times you've heard people say, "I could have done that." A new product like Rollerblades captures consumers' interest and inventors say, "I could have thought of that." A new business like the office-supply company OfficeMax carves out a multimillion-dollar niche in the marketplace and my friends in business say, "I could have done that." And my answer is, "But you didn't." Only action—writing a book, developing a product, launching a business—creates results.

Seize the Moment

Millie Merrill, the owner of a children's clothing store, spotted an opportunity. On windy days, which are all too frequent in Vermont, many customers entered her store looking really, really cold. She saw a need for clothing that would keep people's necks warm on gusty days, so she created Turtle Fur neck warmers. They were such great sellers that she eventually closed her retail store in order to concentrate on growing the neckwear business, Brystie Inc.[1]

Merrill's business idea was innovative, but it would have remained merely a simple theory, an empty form, had she not taken active measures to implement her plan. She gave life to the idea by searching for the best fabrics, creating attractive designs, and developing a manufacturing process. She devoted space in her store for displaying the neck warmers. And she continued her actions by spending more time and energy on the Turtle Fur line as it became increasingly more lucrative.

Lynn Cranmer, a former marathon runner, gave life to her idea and created a successful business when she discovered an unoccupied niche in the market. Frustrated by the lack of good sun visors available in stores, Cranmer started making her own. She had a good idea of what a visor should look like, and she turned that idea into a thriving business. Visors By Lynn generates $500,000 in sales by providing more than thirty kinds of visors for beach, resort, and specialty shops all over the country.[2] But without tangible effort, the idea would never have become a successful business.

Cranmer and Merrill had simple yet novel business ideas. In that respect, these entrepreneurs are a lot like most people. Practically every person I meet has a good business idea. *But what differentiates Cranmer and Merrill from other people is their action characteristic.* Thousands of people have ideas for personal-accessory products, but Cranmer and Merrill acted on their ideas.

The action characteristic also distinguished the great explorers. In 1492, Columbus wasn't the only person who believed the world to be round; neither was he the only person who postulated that the West held vast riches. Many people dreamed of traveling west and finding great wealth, but Columbus was different. "He was the sort of man in whom action is the complement of a dream," writes Samuel Eliot Morison in an essay in the book *The Great Explorers*.[3] What differentiated Columbus from other people of his time was his desire to pursue his vision with concrete, purposeful action.

Columbus was the first to actively attempt the feat of westward exploration. He solicited sponsorship from the king and queen of Spain, learned everything he could about sailing, studied current knowledge of world geography, found the three ships to be used in the journey, formed the expedition team, and equipped the expedition. Columbus realized his dreams and brought Europe into contact with the New World because *he acted on his ideas*.

Barriers to Action

Certainly, preparation is essential to ensure a smooth, successful expedition. But preparation is just a small initial phase in the life of a business.

Many people begin their adventure in the right spirit: they research, study, and acquire relevant skills. Too many people, though, become so engrossed with the preparatory process that they lose sight of the original goal—starting a business.

Others never make it to the preparation stage. Rather than seizing their dreams and taking aggressive steps toward turning theories into reality, they wait for something to happen. Estragon and Vladimir are the ineffectual protagonists of Samuel Beckett's famous play *Waiting for Godot*. Dismissing the rules of Aristotelian tragedy, Beckett constructed a plot line around the *inaction*, rather than the action, of the characters. Estragon and Vladimir do nothing: they stand on a road in the middle of nowhere, waiting for a meeting with a man named Godot. But they're waiting for something that will not happen—Godot never shows up. *Too many people wait for their lives to change rather than make changes in their lives.*

Inactive people often feel that the present moment isn't the right time to take action. For one reason or another, they believe that some point in the future will be a better time to implement their plans. They want to wait until there is more stability in their industry. They want to learn more about the business before they begin. They want to find more startup capital. They want to wait because the children will soon need braces, the holidays are approaching, or the car loan still isn't paid off. There are endless reasons not to act.

But the fact is, it's never the right time. I've learned that conditions will never be as ideal as you would like them to be. The world is in constant flux. Your industry, the economy, your knowledge and skills, and your family are constantly growing and changing. You'll never be able to find a perfectly calm moment when there are no ripples in the water, when you're able to set sail on your journey free from worry. Successful entrepreneurs launch their boats quickly, learn on the journey, and deal with problems as they arise.

Many people are restrained from taking action because they become too complacent—too accepting of their current situations. They comfort themselves with the thought that life isn't so bad at the moment. They get caught up in their daily routines, and their dreams become somewhat removed from everyday life. Life can become easy and comfortable. But inaction and complacency form a seductive trap that pacifies their desire, their will to aggressively seize their dreams.

Many people convince themselves that they'll get the ball rolling on their favorite day—tomorrow. They combine complacency—the dirtiest word in the entrepreneur's vocabulary—with a few excuses, and they've suddenly embraced an old proverb as the chorus of their lives: Never do today what you can put off until tomorrow. But entrepreneurs don't become happy, dynamic, successful people by putting things off. Pros don't procrastinate!

For others, however, procrastination masks a deeper problem. Underneath the waiting, the excuses, and the complacency is a feeling of inadequacy. Some people simply lack the self-confidence necessary to carry out their plans. Procrastination is a way to conceal a lack of belief in the idea, the plan, or the ability to execute it.

These barriers to action can prevent you from taking major actions, like starting a business, and small, day-to-day actions, like purchasing new accounting software or following up on a customer inquiry.

In the jungle of entrepreneurship, thinking and pondering doesn't get you anywhere. Only *acting* moves you closer to your destination.

The mind turns thoughts into ideas,
and action turns ideas into reality.

*Only in men's imagination
does every truth find an
effective and undeniable
existence. Imagination ...
is the supreme master
of art as of life.*

Joseph Conrad (1857–1924)
Ukranian-born English writer

Henry Clay, one of the finest American politicians of the nineteenth century, had quite a vivid imagination. Early in his career, while traveling home from Washington, D.C., the Kentucky statesman stepped down from his carriage. He bent low to the ground and put his ear on the road.

"What are you listening for, Mr. Clay?" his driver asked.

"I am listening," said Clay, "to the unnumbered thousands of feet that will come this way westward."[1]

At that point in U.S. history, few people doubted that Americans would one day inhabit the West. But Clay envisioned not just a migration; he visualized a population explosion. No doubt, his vivid imagination underscored his ability to fashion political compromises between the North and the South that delayed the start of civil war for nearly twenty years.

The Ability to Imagine

Clay's facility in vividly and creatively presenting his vision of the world to others propelled him to political victory. *And it is the same ability to imagine, to envision, that drives many of today's most successful venture adventurers.* Experienced entrepreneurs use their imaginative abilities to create new growth avenues for their businesses, fresh ways to draw customers, and innovative solutions to the many challenges in the jungle of entrepreneurship.

Harry E. Peaden Jr., a Georgia-based entrepreneur, used his creativity to envision an entirely new concept in the meat business. After working only two weeks at a meat-packing company, Peaden "had a wild vision—of Americans hankering for meat delivered to their doorsteps." He quickly made the transition from employee to employer. Peaden launched Country-Fed Meat Company, offering home delivery of the highest-quality beef on the market.

Peaden's imaginative concept has come to life. His company sells fifteen million pounds of steak and poultry door-to-door in thirty states yearly—generating sales of about $65 million.[2] Peaden had his ear pressed close to the ground, and he heard the sounds of meat trucks rolling into the driveways of every home in America! He used his active imagination to envision a new distribution system in an age-old industry.

Creativity also comes in handy in attracting new customers. Les Brown, the former disc jockey turned motivational speaker, tells a terrific story about an exceptionally creative shoeshine boy. Brown was walking down a New York City street, late for a meeting, and he passed four or five shoeshine stands, all staffed by tenacious young men. He was in a hurry, so he declined all their sales pitches. As he crossed the street, he saw yet another young man standing in front of a shoeshine booth, but this one was pointing at people passing by his stand as if he were counting.

As Brown approached, he heard the young man shouting, "96, 97, 98, 99 . . ." Then the young man pointed at Brown and announced exuberantly, "One hundred! Congratulations, sir!" Brown, surprised, stopped and looked at him. And he explained, "Every year on my birthday, I give a free shine to the one-hundredth person that walks by my stand."

Brown, a little skeptical, asked, "Free?"

The young man assured him, "Absolutely!"

Brown looked at his watch and said, "Well, if it's free—go ahead."

He took a seat, and the boy went to work. He cleaned, brushed, and polished. He did a fantastic job. In fact, Brown said that he had never had such a good shoeshine.

So he got up, thanked the young man, said "Happy birthday," and began to walk off. But his conscience stopped him. He turned back and asked, "Listen, how much do you usually charge for a shoeshine?"

"Four dollars," the boy told him.

Brown looked into his wallet, found a ten-dollar bill, and gave it to him, saying, "Hey, you did a great job. Here you go. Have a great birthday." The young man thanked him profusely.

Brown walked away feeling good, and when he was a few strides away, he heard the boy shouting, "96, 97, 98 . . . !"[3]

The young shoeshine boy demonstrated creativity! He used a little imagination and a little ingenuity to increase his revenue in the competitive New York City shoeshine industry.

Chris Whittle, a Tennessee-based entrepreneur, created a multimillion-dollar company by *finding new ways to combine old ideas*—an excellent creative technique in business. He is best known for his innovations in the media business, in which he developed new ways to distribute targeted advertising to the population. For example, he combined the economic strengths of the magazine business with the elegance of book publishing to launch Whittle Publishing. His idea was simple: publish books with advertising pages intermingled among the text.[4] *Whittle has made a fortune creating new venues for advertising by simply combining existing ideas.*

Cultivate Your Creativity

You can cultivate your creativity trait by practicing making new combinations. You can have fun with the simple images you see every day. For instance, you pull up at a stop sign and notice a palm tree on the other side of the street. Here's the creativity exercise: Combine the two images in your brain to form a mental picture of a stop sign bolted to a palm tree. Or you're sitting at your desk eating an apple, and you see a FedEx truck pull up outside your window. So you wonder whether a crate of apples would still be fresh if you shipped it by FedEx to Paris. These kinds of combinations are not just fun mental calisthenics—they force you to think about things in new ways. They are stretching exercises for your brain, and gradually they will help you to think more creatively in business.

Devise ways to use objects for other than their intended purpose. Last summer I witnessed the ultimate example of entrepreneurial creativity. I had just arrived at JFK International Airport in New York. I jumped in a cab to go into the city, but the day was hot and muggy, and traffic around the airport was backed up for miles. I was thirsty! Then along came an entrepreneur selling iced cappuccino. How was he vending iced cappuccino in the middle of a traffic jam? He had a modified pesticide tank—full of iced cappuccino—strapped to his back and a bag of paper cups tied to his waist. I gladly paid two dollars for a cup of this liquid refreshment, as did my cab driver. *This man used his creativity to fill a need!*

Another good exercise to increase your level of creativity is to pose bizarre questions to yourself. Play the "What If" game. For instance, ask yourself what would happen if aliens landed in downtown Seattle tomorrow. Think about this question and stretch your mental muscles. Just think:

- What if marathon runners had to run with a bag of corn chips emptied into their socks?
- What if your city council passed a law that required all chairs to have five legs?
- What if restaurants served just one entrée?

- What if divorce were illegal?
- What if pigs wore athletic shoes?
- What if scientists discovered a way to clone adult human beings?
- What if everyone could travel to the moon as easily as to the corner market?
- What if moving sidewalks made it possible to eliminate cars?
- What if people could hold their breath underwater for five hours at a time?
- What if every person in the world was a citizen of one unified country?

The "What If" game will help you think in new ways and about new things. It will force your brain to stretch, to envision, to conceive, to imagine.

People stifle their creativity by passing judgment on their ideas too quickly. When you're thinking about "What If" questions, imagining new uses for things, or making creative combinations, don't be so quick to evaluate your ideas. Most of what you come up with will be pretty weird; it won't have any practical application to business. But these ideas are the basic building blocks of innovation. Pondering pigs in athletic shoes seems silly, but this kind of mental exercise, when performed regularly, gradually strengthens your creative mind. *So, when ideas show up, let them hang around a while.* Don't allow the pragmatic component of your personality to crush your creative, imaginative ideas before they have had an opportunity to stimulate further thought.

Yes, it's important for you to be sensible, cautious, and practical in your approach to business. But it's also essential to maintain a lighthearted, whimsical, off-the-wall perspective on the world around you. Practicing fun mental exercises enables you to stretch your mind, to enrich your creativity.

The imagination characteristic is acquired slowly, but ultimately the imaginative aspect of your personality will have a profound impact on the success of your venture adventure. Maybe you won't end up selling iced cappuccino from a pesticide tank on your back, but a creative approach to common challenges will bring you uncommon profits.

Your imagination will benefit your expedition
in ways you cannot yet imagine.

PART III

The

Adventure

Principles

The Adventure Principles are the rules of the jungle, the natural laws of the jungle of entrepreneurship. The best entrepreneurs and explorers alike have used them to survive and thrive on their adventures. The explorers may not have realized which of their behaviors brought them prosperity and happiness; they were too busy with the demands of their expeditions to analyze their success systems. But by studying their performances and examining my business experiences, I have delineated ten distinct strategies for achieving successful, enjoyable travel in the jungle of entrepreneurship.

You could launch your expedition without learning the fundamental principles of adventuring. You could set out in search of your treasure with intuition as your only guide and you might succeed. You could be like the Sourdough Expedition, a group of men who attacked North America's tallest mountain, Mt. McKinley, with no plan, inadequate supplies, and almost no knowledge of mountain climbing. "By every accepted standard," writes James R. Ullman in an essay in *The Great Explorers*, "they should not only have made a fiasco of their attempt, but all should have been killed five times over."[1]

They had neither the proper equipment nor the necessary skills, but the members of the Sourdough Expedition successfully scaled the 20,300-foot mountain, which lies 150 miles north of Fairbanks, Alaska. They planted the American flag on the southern peak, leaving evidence of their surprising victory.

The Sourdough men succeeded in part because they had the confidence, courage, and determination necessary to triumph despite their many shortcomings. But the biggest determinant in the fate of their expedition was chance. Sheer luck enabled them to climb and descend without serious injury.

Fortunately, you don't have to rely on luck. Nor do you have to spend years practicing your mountain-climbing technique and studying the journals of other climbers. I've done the hard work for you. The Adventure Principles are proven strategies to help you survive and thrive in the jungle of entrepreneurship. They will guide you from planning and launching your expedition to the everyday events of your venture adventure.

*Learning is not attained
by chance, it must be sought
for with ardor and attended
to with diligence.*

Abigail Adams (1744–1818)
Social critic and first lady of the
United States, 1797–1801

In 1492, when Columbus embarked on an uncertain westward voyage, many of his contemporaries imagined him sailing beyond the Pillars of Hercules, an ancient Greek monument symbolizing the limits of the known world. Fifteenth- and sixteenth-century maps depicted his tiny ship being tossed by towering, sharp waves and surrounded by a host of deadly sea monsters. Most of his contemporaries thought he was a lunatic. He had absolutely no idea what lay beyond the horizon, except for the dangerous, uncertain waters of a cruel ocean and the sea monsters of wild tales conveyed by other mariners.

But Columbus had spent a lot of time *studying and learning* before he set sail and had acquired a vast amount of practical knowledge and useful information. He had thousands of miles of sailing experience from traveling in the Atlantic and down the west coast of Africa. And *he learned all the practical skills* of piloting a ship along the way, including map making, map reading, and navigating by the stars. He also knew the ancient Greek and Latin texts that formed standard educational material in his day, and he was particularly well read in geography and cosmography—so *he knew all the most current theories* about the shape and structure of the earth and its relation to the stars.

Most significant, though, was his experience in the map-making business. Columbus had a thriving chart business that brought him into close contact with all the best mariners of the day, from whom he extracted as much information as he could. *He learned the most up-to-date knowledge* about maps and sketches of the Atlantic, and *he listened carefully to the master mariners* and their stories of distant lands.[1]

If I've learned anything from reading about the world's greatest explorers, it's this: The most critical period of the adventure occurs long before the adventure begins! *The process of learning about the entrepreneurial journey before you begin is the most influential factor in the success of the adventure.* As an astute adventure entrepreneur, you will take the most important steps before you embark on your journey. To equip yourself properly, you must know which are the best provisions for your expedition. To choose the right trail, you must know the topography of the terrain. To find your treasure, you must know how to avoid the mistakes of those who traveled before you.

Columbus didn't become the famous explorer by chance. Yes, he found a continent he had not expected to find, but he couldn't have made the voyage without the proper preparation. He would never have sailed west if he didn't have an intimate knowledge of navigation, geography, and map making. Columbus found success because *he learned the terrain before he embarked.*

Preparation Is All-Important

I've found that Columbus's habit of preparation is also a key to success in the jungle of entrepreneurship. *Learning from the experiences of other entrepreneurs, especially the masters of adventure entrepreneurship, improves your chances for success.* Study the entrepreneurs who have gone before you.

- *Learn from their successes.* Discover what other entrepreneurs have done to develop and improve their enterprises.
- *Learn from their failures.* Study those entrepreneurs who have not been successful, and find out what pitfalls they encountered so you can avoid them.
- *Build upon their experience.* By studying and learning the strategies of other businesspeople, you can gain the benefits of their experience. A potential competitor may have spent an entire year trying to comprehend a certain aspect of the business. You can study that company and learn in one day what took him or her a year to understand.

Livingstone approached his adventures in South Africa with an intense desire to learn. He was so set on preparing himself properly that he isolated himself for about six months. While in seclusion, he acquired an in-depth knowledge of the native language, habits, and thoughts of the people amongst whom he would be traveling. He wrote, "I . . . gained by this ordeal an insight . . . which has proved of incalculable advantage in my intercourse with them ever since."[2] Six months of research and training provided him with a lifetime of information. He continued to reap the benefits of his learning throughout his entire adventure career.

As a general rule, you can gather twenty days of experience in one day of research. In his book *Awaken the Giant Within*, Anthony Robbins writes, "The most powerful way I've learned to compress time is to learn through other people's experience."[3] *Gain the knowledge of your competitors and your predecessors by doing your research. Save yourself time and money by preparing properly.*

That's what Mark David Norris did. As CEO of Send Inc., a progressive greeting-card company, Norris has quickly created a thriving business by showing the same penchant for study, research, and learning that led Columbus toward fame and success.

Norris began with a terrific idea: find a niche in the market by creating fresh, innovative designs as an alternative to the boring, staid greeting cards offered by the major companies. He had in mind a specific design and a specific market. *But rather than launch his expedition without learning the terrain, he embarked on an impressive research campaign.*

He made phone calls to designers and manufacturers throughout the country to learn about printing and distribution. He went to every greeting-card shop he could find and bought, in his words, "every card in sight." He studied the types of paper and the gloss on the cards. He learned as much as he could about the companies he was competing against. *He spent an entire year learning about the industry and studying his competitors.*

Said Norris, "I used our competitors as mentors from a distance." He studied their product lines to benefit from their years of experience. He talked to sales reps and printers to further explore competitors' relationships with customers and suppliers. By going into greeting-card stores and asking customers what they wanted, Norris was able to learn how loyal the customers were to competitors' brands and what niches hadn't yet been filled. He learned which marketing strategies worked well for the other greeting-card companies and which didn't.

Norris told me how excited he had been after visiting the industry's annual greeting-card and stationery show in New York as part of his research. The convention was huge. It took him nearly two days to visit every card stand on the convention floor. Yet he was frustrated with every card design; there was nothing fresh, vibrant, or cutting-edge.

One year later he returned to the same show and debuted his line of greeting cards. His cards were the talk of the show—a huge hit! Before the show Norris had distributed his cards to nine stores; at the show he picked up twenty sales reps. Within a week he had orders from two hundred stores!

Now, three years later, Send Inc. distributes cards to more than 750 stores nationwide. And having just signed contracts with Rizzoli Bookstores and Nordstrom, he estimates that number to reach one thousand shortly. Send Inc. hopes to surpass $1.5 million in sales this year![4]

Norris turned his business idea into a major success *quickly* by doing thorough preparation for his entrepreneurial expedition. Because he studied his competitors, learned from their successes and failures, and invested in the proper research, Send Inc. has experienced tremendous growth. After three years in business, Norris's company is where his major competitors were after eight years of operation, *all because he learned the terrain before he embarked*.

Keep Learning Along the Way

After you've learned everything possible from your research, you're ready to start the adventure. The learning process has taught you how best to equip yourself, which route is the quickest and easiest, and how to avoid possible mistakes along the way. *But the learning process doesn't stop when you embark.* As you journey through the jungle of entrepreneurship, you must continue to learn.

Each time you decide to change direction, you must learn about the new path ahead of you. If you don't know what's beyond the horizon, around the next bend, or past the next thicket of trees, you stand a good chance of running your business aground on a jagged reef or plunging over the edge of a steep ravine. *To sustain the smooth, efficient flow of your expedition, you must be open to change, receptive to new ideas, and above all, willing to engage in continual learning.*

Imagine, for instance, that you've started Frankie's Uptown Deli, a fantastic New York–style delicatessen. You have an ideal storefront location and you've built a strong clientele from the workers in several nearby office buildings. Not only do you serve meals in the restaurant, but also by popular demand you sell jars of mustard with the Frankie's Uptown Deli logo on it. Many customers buy the product as gifts. You've been open for almost a year, and each month sales have steadily improved. Your venture adventure has been a complete success so far.

Like the best explorers, you're looking constantly for new ways to improve your expedition. You want to maintain your current growth rate by branching into new directions. You've heard about direct mail—the ads, coupons, and letters of solicitation sent through the mail—and you want to try it. "What an excellent way," you think, "to increase revenue. I'll sell the Frankie's Uptown Deli mustard product through the mail!" It sounds like a great idea. Theoretically, Frankie's mail-order division can sell the mustard to deli-lovers all over America—a huge market! After all, companies like Lands' End and Harry & David have multizillion-dollar businesses selling products through the mail. So you jump right in with both feet.

But you don't do the proper preparation. You don't take the time to find out if your idea has worked for your competitors, and you don't stop to think if it will work for you. You never find out that direct mail is a very delicate, risky venture. It is, in fact, a science. Direct mail is a big gamble because the cost of mailing all those advertisements is enormous and only a very small percentage of people ever respond. But you don't learn this until it's too late. You invest $50,000 of the company's $100,000 cash reserves in the direct-mail effort, and you get orders for thirteen jars of mustard.

You just ran your business against a jagged reef and tore a huge hole into the hull of your ship. Although you haven't ruined the expedition, your business has suffered a serious setback.

Mark Cohn, co-founder of the Damark catalog company, knows the value of continual learning. He started his company in 1986 with $1,000; eight years later it grossed $364 million in sales! Cohn not only created a prosperous business from scratch, but he continues to ensure its success by constantly learning about his business. In a recent article in *Inc.*, Cohn described his attitude toward entrepreneurship:

> For me, the challenge has been, What do I need to learn to lead this business into its next stage? What do I need to know? What don't I know? What haven't I thought about? Where can I get that information? The great joy in this job is not to create value, which we've done, or to be well compensated, which we are; the joy is in the ability to learn.[5]

Cohn is truly alive with the spirit of entrepreneurship. Although he likes seizing the treasure, most of all he enjoys the thrill of the adventure. *He doesn't live for the money; he lives for the challenge—the challenge of constantly learning, of continually searching for new ways to make his business more successful.*

Apply Your Learning

Peary was a man of action. He made several expeditions into the Arctic and Antarctic; like other master explorers, he did his homework before he embarked and continued to learn during his expeditions.

During one campaign, Peary devoted time each day to making plans for a new ship. He wrote, "I began plans for another ship of the same general size and model of the *Roosevelt* for Arctic or Antarctic work but with improvements and details modified in the light of experience gained . . . ."[6] So he would not forget what he learned daily on the expedition, he created a detailed description of his next ship by using his knowledge gained each day.

By converting his experiences into practical wisdom that could be used to build a new ship, Peary made excellent use of what he was learning. As you sail along on *your* business adventure, make use of *your* learning by altering your ship or even by building a new ship if you must.

Some of the most successful adventurers in the jungle of entrepreneurship have applied their knowledge and their penchant for continual learning by building a new ship in midadventure. You've heard of Bill Gates, founder and CEO of Microsoft and today the wealthiest person in America. But you may not know of Gates's friend and one-time business associate Kuzuhiko "Kay" Nishi. Computer salesman Nishi spearheaded Microsoft's push into the Asian personal-computer market. Then Nishi redefined the art of shipbuilding.

From the beginning of their relationship, Gates and Nishi had been extremely close, each sharing the same energy and enthusiasm about the computer-software business. Both men were highly skilled and very ambitious, and business together was a tremendous success: their partnership was making millions upon millions of dollars for them both. Nishi, standing at the wheel of the Microsoft ship, sailed smoothly along, riding a tidal wave of success through the software jungle. Why, then, did he decide to jump overboard and climb to the helm of another?

He believed that his current ship would be inadequate for further adventures. Nishi, exhibiting the best learning skills of the most successful explorers, kept his thumb pressed closely to the pulse of computer technology. He possessed an intimate knowledge of the industry, and he sensed that trends were changing, that semiconductor chips were the next hot opportunity. Nishi wanted to go with chips; Gates wouldn't budge from software. (In fact, both the chip and the software markets proved incredibly lucrative in the following decade.) So Nishi harnessed his knowledge. He broke away from Microsoft to devote full-time attention to his own company, ASCII. Nishi became a hero in Japan. ASCII became Japan's largest software company and the publisher of many of the nation's most popular magazines.[7]

Your Knowledge Is Your Greatest Asset

Look over this balance sheet for Dandy Candy Inc., owned and run by entrepreneur and candy connoisseur Bubba Gum.

Dandy Candy Inc.
Balance Sheet

Assets		*Liabilities*	
Cash	$ 30,000	Accounts payable	$ 10,000
Building	62,000	Owners' equity	112,000
Accounts receivable	9,000		
Inventory	21,000		
Total assets	$122,000	Total liabilities	$122,000

Notice that liabilities are listed in the right-hand column. Take a look at the assets on the left. You'll see that the form provides listings for Dandy Candy's cash accounts, property, accounts receivable, and inventory. But nowhere on this balance sheet can you find a listing for the company's greatest asset: the owner's *knowledge, skill, and experience.*

As founder and owner of your company, you possess more complete knowledge of the business than anyone! The adventure has been yours from the beginning. You did all the research: you learned from the successes and failures of your competitors, and you acquired the value of their experience. You equipped the expedition, and you gave it a unique identity on the high seas. You continued to improve and develop the company by continuing to learn along the way.

Just ask Sol Price how valuable the owner's knowledge of the business is to the company's success. After seventeen years as a practicing attorney, Price decided to trade the comfort and security of a steady, well-paying job for a revitalizing adventure in the jungle of entrepreneurship. You may know him as the founder of Price Club (or Price-Costco, after the merger), the nationwide chain of discount warehouse stores. However, Price began his career in business when he started Fed-Mart, a chain of supermarkets that specialized in private-label brands. Price sold Fed-Mart to a West

German buyer. In what turned out to be an enormous mistake for the new owner, Price was fired from the company he built. The loss of this invaluable resource was too much for the business to withstand. Fed-Mart failed.[8] Price was the life-blood of the company—it couldn't survive without him.

No one is more important than you, the owner, to the success of the company. You are your company's greatest asset. You belong on the balance sheet, because the company can buy more inventory or construct a new building, but it cannot replace you! An accurate balance sheet for Dandy Candy would look like this:

Dandy Candy Inc.
True Balance Sheet

Assets		Liabilities	
Cash	$ 30,000	Accounts payable	$ 10,000
Building	62,000	Owner's equity	112,000+
Accounts receivable	9,000	($112,000 plus the priceless value	
Inventory	21,000	of the owner's knowledge)	
Bubba Gum	priceless		
Total assets	$122,000	Total liabilities	$122,000

When big corporations buy smaller companies and when banks evaluate businesses for credit, the *true* balance sheet is never examined. That is why sales and profits often decrease after a company is purchased by a large conglomerate. Without the owner at the helm, the company is ineffective. Also, loan officers pay far too much attention to the regular asset and liability items and frequently fail to evaluate the value of the entrepreneur to the business. They may reject a loan application for lack of collateral, failing to realize that the entrepreneur's experience and knowledge justify an unsecured loan.

The privilege of being the ship's captain is accompanied by tremendous responsibility. Because you alone have the ability, you are, above all others, responsible for keeping the ship afloat. I maintain a regular learning program to ensure that my businesses, as well as the clients of my consulting company, are benefiting from the most current knowledge about entrepreneurship. It includes the following.

Reading books and magazines. When I visit bookstores and libraries, I am amazed by the amount of resources available to entrepreneurs. Read *Entrepreneur, Inc.,* and *Business Week* for general trends in entrepreneurship and business; also read *Nation's Business*, a less well known but often insightful magazine. Check newspapers for daily, hot information about new developments and opportunities. *The Wall Street Journal*'s "Marketplace" section frequently contains pertinent stories about small business, as does *USA Today*'s "Money" section. (I receive and read three newspapers every weekday.) For more specialized information on your industry, talk to other entrepreneurs and search for magazines, journals, and newsletters devoted specifically to your field. Check the library for books and other reference materials that may prove helpful.

Listening to speakers. Attend seminars, conferences, and presentations. Every event I attend provides me with significant knowledge and insight. It's also a great way to become acquainted with the major players in your field and to find out what's on the cutting edge of your industry.

Listening to audiotapes. Recently there has been a boom in audiotape publishing. Today you can find an incredible variety of material on audio-tape, including taped books on business and personal development. Tapes are great if you don't have much time to read. You can listen to them while you exercise, cook dinner, clean the house, or drive. If you spend thirty minutes a day in the car, you'll spend about eleven thousand hours of your life on the road. In comparison, a four-year college education consists of about two thousand hours of instruction. Use your time in the car to attend Commuter University and graduate with more than five bachelor's degrees!

Learning is at the foundation of all successful enterprises. The world's greatest explorers were educated individuals who made learning a lifetime endeavor, never ceasing to pursue knowledge. You, too, must dedicate your-self to a lifetime of learning, both before and during each expedition, to journey successfully through the jungle of entrepreneurship.

> *Learning and achieving are infinitely intertwined.*
> *The more you learn, the more you achieve,*
> *and the more you achieve, the more you learn.*

*It is thrifty to prepare today
for the wants of tomorrow.*   Aesop

After you carry out the necessary research and learn everything possible about the adventure you are about to embark upon, you'll be ready to equip yourself. This is the time when you'll gather all the physical supplies you will need to help you manage the difficult terrain, contend with possible pitfalls and traps, and arrive safely at the treasure.

There are plenty of big decisions to make. Fortunately, though, I have plenty of good advice! First, *equipping yourself well doesn't mean packing as much gear as possible—it means packing the right gear*. If you've researched your adventure well, it shouldn't be difficult for you to decide which materials to include on your equipment list and which to exclude.

After you decide on a specific list of absolutely necessary materials, you'll want to keep two things in mind. *As a general rule, bring enough supplies for a journey that may take twice as long as you expect*. Your journey may be wild and uncertain, so prepare yourself for the unexpected by packing more than you'll need. Secondly, however, *be very careful not to overpack*.

These rules translate into a money issue. You must be very careful with the capital you've obtained—whether from personal funds or a bank loan—to start your venture. Too many times I've seen entrepreneurs spend money recklessly and carelessly. Obviously, you'll need this money to purchase the physical supplies you'll need to start your business—perhaps a computer, phone, desk, and the like. But you'll also need it for other uses, some of which are as vital to your business as canned food is to an expedition.

The Three Kinds of Supplies

As you develop a catalog of items you'll need, you'll soon notice that not all supplies are equal. *Some are more necessary than others*, and it will be important for you to understand which kinds of equipment you'll need first, which you can expect to gather along the way (and how to do it), and which may seem expendable but are, in fact, very necessary.

The following three kinds of supplies will help you identify which deserve high priority on your shopping list and which can wait until later.

The bare necessities. These supplies sustain your day-to-day operations; they are absolutely essential to the basic function of your expedition, for without them you can go no further. These needs must be fulfilled before you can concentrate on the remainder of your equipment list.

A good way to think about this concept is by comparing it to Abraham Maslow's hierarchy of needs. Maslow, a psychologist, suggested that human beings are driven to act by a variety of needs which are organized in a pyramid-shaped hierarchy. He hypothesized that basic physiological needs, such as hunger and thirst, lay at the bottom and that subsequent layers consist of safety needs, love needs, esteem needs, cognitive needs, desire for aesthetic experience, and finally, self-actualization needs.

The idea is that the needs which lie at the bottom must be satisfied before subsequent needs can be fulfilled. That is, after we have averted the distractions of hunger and thirst, which are at the bottom, we progress toward a new set of needs, including the need for physical safety. And each time the needs of a level are met, we ascend to the next level. We hope to eventually reach the highest level: self-actualization needs, those pertaining to finding self-fulfillment and to realizing our potential.[1]

Your business also operates within a hierarchy of needs. Its most basic needs are the supplies you will need to sustain its daily operation. These needs must be satisfied first. If your business requires an office setup, items such as a computer, fax machine, and telephone must be secured before you can begin to equip yourself with more supplies. Until such bare necessities are obtained, don't purchase the black marble art deco coffee table on display at your local furniture store.

All businesses, regardless of their size and irrespective of the kinds of goods and services they supply, share the most basic of all necessities: cash flow. *For a business, cash is food.* I've come to believe that a young business eats like a young elephant: as soon as it finishes one large meal, it is ready for another. As a part of your expedition's basic equipment, ready sums of money will be the most significant asset. Not only will you spend this money to purchase the bare necessities of your operation, but you will use it to establish your business (product development, advertising, etc.). Eventually, your profitable business will provide most of your cash flow.

But until your company begins to generate cash, your cash flow will come from your original startup funds.

Tools to gather food along the trail. A good way to minimize the size of your equipment list is to pack devices that will help you gather more supplies as you journey toward the treasure. For instance, you don't have to pack food for the entire journey if you bring a fishing rod that will help you obtain food along the way.

Some of the world's greatest explorers applied this principle with amazing ingenuity. Members of the *Kon Tiki* raft expedition, for example, went to great lengths to replenish their water supply. Because they traveled on a raft at sea for a long time, they had to consider their drinking needs. They might have packed large canisters of fresh water, but storage space was minimal and too many supplies would have diminished the raft's buoyancy. They solved their problem by collecting water from natural rainfall and by extracting the juice from raw fish, of which there was an endless supply.[2] They used their ingenuity and creativity to gather supplies during their journey rather than embark with everything they needed for the entire trip.

Livingstone, too, learned how to gather food along the trail. In a manner no less ingenious than that of the members of the *Kon Tiki*, Livingstone discovered how to gather food "in the driest parts of the desert, where to an ordinary observer there is not a sign of life." From the Bushmen, he learned that the Matlametlo frog, which looks and tastes like chicken when cooked, digs a hole at the foot of a particular bush and rests there during dry spells. By looking beneath spiderwebs, which usually covered the openings to the frogs' holes, Livingstone was able to gather plenty of food where seemingly none existed.[3]

The ability to procure supplies for yourself along the trail will prove to be vital to your success. Cash is the most important tool in this respect. If you begin with $10,000, you can use this money skillfully to create $100,000 and then $1 million. A strong cash flow is beneficial in two ways. It allows you to finance the growth of your business *and* to draw money from the business. (Lest we forget, profiting is one of the main goals of starting a business.) Bring cash—the valuable tool—on your adventure, and you will find that supplies never run short.

I learned the value and the importance of a strong cash flow from one of the master business adventurers of our day, Kay Nishi. I chatted with Nishi at a recent World Economic Forum summit in Switzerland, eager to know how one of Japan's richest and most successful businessmen created his computer-software empire. "Kay," I asked him, "what is the most important business strategy you would share with a beginning entrepreneur?"

His reply was simple. Expressionless, he looked me in the eye and deadpanned, "Cash flow." Then his face brightened into a smile, and he said, "Then you can buy a helicopter, and also keep your business growing!"

You see, Nishi's favorite toy is his helicopter. This flamboyant businessman loves to travel by helicopter whenever possible. *And as long as he maintains a strong cash flow in his businesses, he's able to withdraw plenty of that money as profit.* Because he created businesses with strong cash flows, he can afford his expensive tastes.

But more important, cash flow can be used to finance the growth of your business. I developed and improved my businesses by following Nishi's advice. I created a stronger cash flow for the companies by improving the accounts-receivable operations. I simplified and streamlined the billing processes. Today invoices are paid in about half the time they used to take, which keeps accounts receivable low and provides more available cash. With this money on hand, I can seize the opportunities for growth as they appear.

The availability of ready sums of money is critical to the success of your business as well as to your personal life. Nishi and his helicopter attest to that. But this idea has been around for a long time. Benjamin Franklin, a man noted for his frugality, industry, and good common sense, described ready money as one of the faithful friends in life. This wisdom is just as relevant today as it was when Franklin voiced it in 1736. *No friend will be more faithful to you in the jungle of entrepreneurship than the ready money created by a strong cash flow.*

Luxury items. These supplies are not absolutely necessary, but they are highly desirable, for they will make your journey much easier and more pleasant. The need for these items lies near the top level of Maslow's hierarchy of motives. *Although they are not must-have items, they do play a significant role in the success of your business.* But consider carefully the luxury items you'll want to bring with you.

On a jungle expedition, such items may consist of spices for cooking, pillows, and musical instruments. These items will not play a part in the daily function of the campaign, nor will they help to gather more supplies along the trail. But they will contribute to the smoothness and efficiency of your campaign in less tangible ways.

Luxury items will have the same effect on your business. *Equipping yourself with simple, sometimes inexpensive items can have a terrific effect on company morale*. If you purchase padded chairs with strong lower-back support, your office workers will be able to sit comfortably for longer periods of time and produce acceptable work more quickly and efficiently.

When equipping yourself for the adventure, keep in mind that small luxury items can sometimes be of great practical value. After meeting the basic biological needs of your business and making plans to gather more supplies along the trail, make room for a few items that will make significant contributions to company spirit and morale.

Packing Your Supplies

After you've decided which supplies will best accompany you, you'll need to decide how to pack them. You may not have given much thought to this aspect of the journey, but it is an important task and should not be taken lightly. Some of the best explorers have caused themselves serious misfortune by not packing supplies properly. Let us learn from their mistakes and pack our supplies effectively.

Hsuan-Tsang, a Chinese monk who traveled throughout Asia in the seventh century, encountered significant difficulties by not packing his supplies properly. As he advanced through the Gobi desert, Hsuan-Tsang rationed his water carefully. Unfortunately, though, he lost his way and then further compounded his problems by losing his water supply. One of the monk's students wrote of the episode, "When he was going to drink from the pipe of his water-vessel, because of its weight it slipped from his hands, and the water was wasted; thus, a supply enough for a thousand li [300 miles] was lost in a moment."[4]

Lost in the desert with no water, Hsuan-Tsang was in serious life-threatening danger. Fortunately, he made it out of the desert, but not after experiencing plenty of hardship and suffering. If he had packed his water in several smaller containers, however, he could have prevented the loss of his entire supply.

Avoid potential disaster by packing supplies carefully. You may want to distribute your most important supplies into smaller packages. For example, if you plan to operate a business that will require you to store a great deal of information on a computer, you may want to store it in several areas or on backup disks. This way, if a power surge or a bug in the system destroys your files, your entire operation won't be lost. Perhaps you plan to run a retail business in which you will keep large amounts of cash in your registers. You may think about making several cash deposits throughout the day, instead of only one at the end of the day, to safeguard the money against theft. Disburse your supplies and reduce the potential for disaster.

The Challenge of Undercapitalization

Frank W. Barton, an entrepreneur from Kansas, made a fortune in the rent-to-own industry. He founded the Rent-a-Center chain of stores. After I gave a speech in Wichita, Mr. Barton and I had a talk, and he gave me some good advice about starting businesses. "Daryl, I've never seen a business that has been overcapitalized. You see, not having enough money is part of the challenge every entrepreneur faces. That's what makes starting businesses interesting."

The significance of his comment hit me like a freight train. I had always been annoyed by not having enough startup funds for some ventures. *No business ever has enough capital to grow properly*, and banks will lend you money only if you can prove you don't need it! No entrepreneur starts out with as much capital as she or he would like. There always seems to be a short supply of cash, but it is normal and is part of the adventure.

Consider what happened to Dana Sinkler and Alex Dzieduszycki, founders of Terra Chips, makers of a new, exotic vegetable snack-chip line. Their business was growing at a phenomenal rate, and everyone was talking about their product. (Who could resist talking about Coriander Spiced Taro Chips and Cayenne Pepper Spiced Sweet Potato Chips?) In two years their sales rocketed from about $600,000 to $3 million, nearly a 500 percent increase!

Even with extraordinary growth numbers, these entrepreneurs had trouble getting capital. They applied for a loan from a prominent bank to purchase larger office space and more production materials. They needed cash to help them keep pace with the rapid growth of their hot business. But the bank turned them down. Terra Chips eventually got the money. In a complex array of business and political maneuvers, they were able to secure a credit line.[5]

No one ever promised that acquiring capital would be easy. Money is always hard to come by, but that's what makes entrepreneurship exciting. If it were easy to acquire startup capital, starting a business wouldn't be an adventure.

One challenge of business is to turn a little money into a lot of money. Starting with a limited supply of capital shouldn't be considered a deficiency; it's a challenge that makes the whole adventure worthwhile. Don't let a perceived shortage of capital stop you from beginning your venture adventure.

Ask Frank Barton. He and his partner started Rent-a-Center with $20,000—$10,000 each—and sold it twelve years later for somewhere in the range of half a billion dollars! Barton accepted the challenge, turned a little into a lot, and proved that you *don't* have to have millions to make millions.

Remember: As you gather all the supplies you'll need on your adventure, do first things first. Take special care with your startup capital. Use it wisely to purchase the "biological" needs of your outfit, use the rest to help you gather supplies along the way, and package your materials carefully so as not to allow a small disaster to throw you off course.

A can of sardines may satisfy your appetite for a day;
a fishing pole can satisfy your appetite for a lifetime.

*In the long run men hit
only what they aim at.*

Henry David Thoreau (1817–1862)
American writer

Some experienced adventurers trekked across the African plains with an elephant gun in hand. They led expeditions composed of several guides, a crew of a dozen people, and hundreds of pounds of supplies. They packed much gear and they hunted big game: lions, tigers, and elephants.

Other hunters worked alone. Packing only what could be carried easily on a day's hike, they traveled lightly. Their adventure was uncomplicated, flexible, and easy to manage. They usually packed a shotgun: a short-range weapon that fires small, scattered pellets. The gun is powerful but is used mainly for small game, like rabbit, pheasant, and turkey.

The biggest difference between these two kinds of hunters was not the size of the guns they carried. It was not the size of their outfits, how much gear they packed, or the number of people working for them. The real difference between them was what was visible in their gun sights. *What distinguished them was the targets at which they aimed!*

Think about it: Both did essentially the same amount of work. Both were extremely knowledgeable about the animals to be hunted. Both knew the terrain. Both spent the entire day covering ground and pursuing prey. The only significant distinction was the size of the animal they hunted.

Thankfully, in most East African countries, hunting big game has been illegal for many years. Although I oppose hunting as a sport, I believe the big game/small game analogy is very effective in helping you develop your business goals. *The only difference between a small business and a large business is the target in sight.* The owner of a small business performs many of the same tasks as does the CEO of a large corporation. Both work twelve hours a day learning, thinking of ways to improve the operation, overseeing employees, controlling production costs, and talking to customers. The CEO, however, is shooting for a sales figure much higher than the proprietor of the small business.

If you own and run a small business, you're already doing the same kind of work as your corporate counterparts do—and doing it in the same amount of time. So, if you're going to hunt, why not hunt big game? Why not shoot for $1 million in sales instead of $100,000? *If you don't aim high, you won't score big.*

Throughout his lifetime, Thoreau challenged himself to attain the full capacity of his power as an individual living within a free society. He believed that the only way to realize his full potential was to continually ask more of himself: he could achieve perfection only if he aimed for perfection. If you don't strive for maximum potential, you'll never achieve it. Have the courage to challenge yourself. This is beginning to sound like a commercial for the Air Force, but *I believe in the power of aiming high*.

The founders of Lone Star Steak Houses, a Wichita-based chain of steak restaurants, aimed high from the beginning and never looked down. Most small restaurant owners expect to gross $200,000 to $500,000 a year if they want to take home some decent profits. Not the managers of Lone Star, however. They have different expectations. They set goals of $3 million a year for each of their restaurants, and they reach it. The menu pricing is comparable to other restaurants in their class, and they operate in about the same amount of square footage, so functionally they aren't much different from their competitors. The food is excellent and the service is top-notch, but that doesn't really account for the fact that their per-store revenues exceed those of their competitors by more than 600 percent.

What really separates the Lone Star founders from the rest of the crowd is their vision. If they thought like most entrepreneurs, they probably would have been content with much lower figures. Even $1 million would have been double what other good restaurants gross, but they went higher than that.

I know what you're thinking. Three million dollars in sales seems an outrageous goal. Maybe even $1 million in sales is a bit much for your landscaping business, drugstore, or plumbing-supplies center. But what's the worst that can happen by aiming high? You miss?

Let's say you own and operate three small laundromats. Each does approximately $35,000 a year in sales, for a total of $105,000. This year, though, your expectations are higher. You decide to set your sights on $500,000 in total sales, which is roughly $166,000 per store—an increase of almost 500 percent.

In a furious effort to meet this goal, you launch a no-holds-barred advertising campaign: commercials on the radio; large, colorful ads in the Sunday paper; and bigger, more attractive signs in front of each store. You revamp the interior design of the stores with a few coats of paint and some comfortable living-room furniture (which you buy cheap at a used-furniture store). Your customers will certainly be more comfortable lounging on the soft furniture than the cold, hard cafeteria-style chairs you had. You install vending machines in the three locations to further increase sales.

But you fall well short of your $500,000 goal. You gross only $300,000. But that's nearly triple your previous annual sales! *You've missed the mark, but by aiming high you've improved considerably.*

If you aim high and fail to reach the goals you've set for yourself and your company, you'll still go a long way. I heard author Les Brown say it best: "Aim for the moon, and if you miss you'll hit a star!"[1]

The Five Levels of Distribution

Aiming for the big game is important, but equally important is choosing a quarry appropriate to your experience and background. If you were a seasoned hunter and knew how to handle an elephant rifle, then perhaps you'd be ready for a full-blown safari. But if you have little experience in the field, then you'll want to start small and *work your way up.*

I have identified five levels of distribution that should help you choose an appropriate place to begin your hunt. These levels roughly correspond to a hierarchy of business classes that range from small to large. Create a set of intermediate goals in which you begin on a small level and work your way to the top by moving through one level at a time.

Begin by choosing a level on which you feel comfortable. Let your amount of experience and specialized knowledge in a particular industry help you decide. After you've developed your business on a given level, move to the next one by expanding your field of vision. Start small, but think big!

The local level. This is the smallest level. It applies to your neighborhood and the area immediately surrounding your business. On this level, goods and services rarely flow outside the community, so your product or service is designed primarily for the neighborhood in which you've set up shop. For example, a small hair salon that caters mainly to people who live nearby operates on the local level.

The city level. This is slightly larger than the local level. The businesses that operate in this class serve a wider customer base and distribute goods over a larger area. For instance, a baker who owns a small factory and distributes cakes, breads, and pastries to grocery stores and restaurants in the city operates on this level. If you know the terrain and demographics of your city quite well, you should be comfortable starting on the city level.

The state level. This is a larger, more sophisticated level involving a wider transportation of goods and services and a significantly larger customer base. You can move up to this level by adding a store in another city or by shipping your baked goods to other cities in your state.

The national level. National distribution entails providing goods and services to customers across the country. But you don't necessarily have to open locations in other parts of the country to operate on this level. With a toll-free number, fax machine, and overnight delivery services, you can work with customers 5,000 miles away as easily as those next door.

The international level. You may be suited to begin an international business if you have experience in a corporation with international offices, speak several languages, know a particular foreign culture very well, or have excellent contacts in other countries. Otherwise, start a business on one of the other levels and move up to the international level. If you make and sell cookies, for instance, first put them on shelves in your city, then your state, then across the nation, and finally, in Canada or Mexico or even in England and France. If you do the baking and packaging in Ames, Iowa, you can ship them to London as easily as you can to Louisville.

Advancing Through the Levels

Keep in mind that these levels of distribution are rough guidelines. Use them to approximate your advance toward the big game. Michael Gerber, author of *The E Myth*, has created a fantastic system that will help you move easily through the levels. His concept asks that you think of your business as the prototype of thousands of businesses yet to be created. You'll want to simplify and perfect your model business in every way possible down to the smallest detail.[2]

For example, if you own a restaurant, perfect its operation and simplify *everything* so that it can be easily duplicated. Pay attention to the interior and exterior design, including the landscaping, the shape of the building, the floor plans, and even the pictures and other artwork decorating the interior. The menus should be identical, as should the placement of silverware on the tables. Formulate a standard system of food ordering, nightly bookkeeping, and waste disposal. *Standardize everything.* Create a uniform for employees, and have them recite a specific greeting to each guest who walks through the front door. Eventually, customers in Atlanta, Boston, and San Francisco will hear the same words come from their host or hostess.

After you've perfected the standards of your operation and have simplified every aspect of the business, you're ready to duplicate it. You turn on your business-copying machine! You begin by opening your restaurants in other areas of the city, then in different parts of the state. When you feel comfortable on this level, you open duplicate restaurants in every part of the nation. Even as your business grows, you keep thinking bigger. You can move quickly through the levels of distribution by *duplicating your business*.

Gerber also has wonderful advice that will help you manage your business as you lead it through the levels of distribution: "Work *on* your business, not *in* it."[3] Spend your time and energy focusing on ways to improve and develop your operation, not on the minor details of its day-to-day affairs.

The Successive-Mountain Concept

Thinking big and aiming high, though, isn't the whole story. The successful entrepreneurs I've met all agree: Aiming for the moon is a good start, but the secret to extraordinary accomplishment is continually readjusting your sights, aiming higher and higher. *To be successful on your journey, you must continue to think bigger and bigger with each step, establishing new goals when you reach each plateau.*

I like to call this idea the *successive-mountain concept.* If you've aimed for the big game and hit your target, then you've done well for yourself. You've achieved your goal. Mission accomplished. Congratulations. Now you're standing at the top of the mountain. And the view is breathtaking as you watch the green and brown expanse beneath you. The clouds appear as trophies. The sun bends close to congratulate you on a job well done.

But rest easy in the adulation for only a moment. *Look carefully and you will see another, taller mountain just off in the distance.* In fact, you'll notice that there is an infinite succession of mountains, each waiting to be conquered. Successful explorers and prosperous entrepreneurs alike will readjust their sights and head for the next peak.

As a true adventure entrepreneur, each time you set a goal and achieve it, you will naturally begin to formulate another goal. Do not become complacent. Keep striving higher and higher. Challenge yourself to continue to develop and improve. The only way to become successful is to raise your sights, and the only way to remain successful is to keep raising them.

> ***You will hit that at which you aim,
> so aim at something you want to take home.***

CHAPTER 13

When You Encounter a Ravine, Build a Bridge

The New Frontier of which I speak is not a set of promises—it is a set of challenges.

John F. Kennedy (1917–1963)
Thirty-fifth president of the United States

A lone adventurer, machete in hand, slashes his way through dense jungle foliage. He's moving quickly. The precious gems he's been searching for lie in a cave not far away. His hat is pulled down low to protect his face from the wild undergrowth, and his eyes scan the ground immediately in front of him. He's picking up speed, moving faster, getting closer.

Suddenly, a two-hundred-foot ravine appears out of nowhere, hidden by the thick jungle trees. Were it not for his quick reflexes, his next step could have been his last!

What does he do? The ravine is too wide to jump, too steep to climb, and too long to walk around. Does he give up and turn around? Does he become angry, shaking his fists in the air and cursing his incompetent mapmaker? Does he turn in circles, frightened, desperate, and uncertain?

No! He sits back and surveys the situation. He calmly reviews his options and decides on a plan. He fashions a rope from vines growing on the jungle floor and heaves it across the gorge, creating a simple, makeshift bridge. He scrambles across the wide expanse without much difficulty. Little time is wasted and the treasure is still within his grasp. Resourcefulness and determination have served him well.

In spite of your best-laid plans, and no matter how well you've equipped yourself, unforeseen obstacles will probably arise. Even a well-planned journey will most likely encounter an unexpected hurdle. *There is no guarantee of a safe, smooth ride through the jungle of entrepreneurship!*

Peary talked about his struggles: "There are . . . so many trump cards which can be played against him who attempts to do serious work in the highest latitudes, that there is always some vital point which in spite of every care and provision and forethought threatens to go wrong."[1] Peary understood that when an explorer undertakes a serious venture, problems will inevitably arise, no matter how well the trip was planned.

Expect Challenges

As you explore the higher latitudes of business, you can expect to encounter unanticipated obstacles. Pitfalls in the jungle of entrepreneurship can assume any number of shapes and sizes. You may have a small problem with the invoice printer in your distribution warehouse, which is further complicated when the repairer who was supposed to show up yesterday still doesn't come today. Or you may have larger problems. Perhaps an electrical fire destroys three-fourths of your inventory. Or maybe winter never hits hard this year and your snowplowing business takes a beating. You never know what hurdle may be thrust in your path next.

But when explorers encounter obstacles, they create solutions. Peary eventually made it to the North Pole. As an entrepreneur, you, too, must rely on your resourcefulness and determination to create solutions to the problems, obstacles, and misfortunes that come your way.

The Great Ross Ice Barrier

Now, I know what you're thinking. Obstacles can sometimes seem like impossibly large impediments on the road to success. Sometimes there is nothing you can do: certain obstacles seem totally insurmountable.

Expect adversity. Hidden obstacles are a natural part of the jungle terrain. Even the narrowest straits, the deepest canyons, the fiercest rapids can be conquered. Experienced adventure entrepreneurs know that extremely daunting challenges occur all the time in business. Huge obstacles are not unusual. Expect to encounter a towering hurdle every few months as well as the small daily snares.

Take James Ross, for example. This British explorer spent months braving the harsh elements of Antarctica while attempting to reach the South Pole before he was finally halted by a gigantic ice barrier. Ross described this intimidating force as "an obstruction of such character as to leave no doubt upon my mind as to our future proceedings, for we might with equal chance of success try to sail through the cliffs of Dover, as penetrate such a mass."[2]

Ross found this obstacle too difficult to overcome. Though he attempted to penetrate farther south, he never managed to reach the South Pole. The obstacle was eventually known as the Ross Ice Barrier.

But what seemed like an insurmountable obstacle to Ross was an opportunity for someone else. Seventy years after Ross was turned back by the ice barrier, another explorer turned it into an advantage by traveling directly over it to reach the South Pole.

Don't let your obstacles become someone else's opportunity. Often, what seems like an insurmountable barrier is really a challenge. Prior to FedEx, there was only one way to ensure that a package would arrive at its destination the following morning: You put a messenger on a plane. Upon arriving in the destination city, the messenger would hand-deliver the package to the recipient and call to inform you of the delivery time. Of course, this method was rather expensive!

Fred Smith, the founder of FedEx, first thought of the idea for his company in an economics class. He proposed a spoke distribution system, in which planes from cities across the United States would fly into Memphis, Tennessee, in the middle of the night. Packages would be removed from the incoming planes, routed through a sorting center, and then loaded onto outgoing planes. This ingenious system eliminated the cost of flying planes directly from city to city.

Smith's business professor at Yale gave him a C on his economics paper! But undaunted by this criticism, Smith persevered and turned his simple idea into a business that has truly changed our lives.

Use *your* resourcefulness and determination to turn unexpected obstacles into fantastic opportunities for *you* and *your expedition*. Don't allow an ice barrier to be named after you!

Pull Your Canoes Out of the River

Sometimes the best way to solve a problem is to move around it. As you embark on your business adventure, you will find that it is easy to become spellbound by the aggressive, adventuresome spirit of entrepreneurship. You'll want to grab every bull by the horns and wrestle it to the ground. However, tackling a problem head-on is not always the best solution.

When Livingstone took his expedition down a South African river, he encountered the Falls of Gonye—a dangerous thirty-foot drop littered with jagged rocks. Wisely, he opted not to confront the obstacle head-on. Instead, he chose to remove his canoes from the river and to carry them around the falls to a safer spot downstream.[3]

Some adventurers, carelessly overconfident, would have braved the Falls of Gonye. They would have risked everything and most likely would have lost. The first solution—attacking the falls—was not the best solution. Because Livingstone was levelheaded, thought carefully, and exercised good judgment, he made it downstream safely. *He succeeded because he moved around the obstacle instead of moving through it.*

Often, there are solutions or options more practical and more feasible than the ones that immediately come to mind. And clear, objective thinking is the key to finding them. Making the right decisions—choosing to attack a problem boldly or opting to slide smoothly around it—requires you to be cautious.

Thoreau said, "It is characteristic of wisdom not to do desperate things." One prominent trait of wisdom is the ability to think and act rationally.

You don't have to meet all the Ross Ice Barriers and all the Falls of Gonye with the desperate actions of a person with no options. I've seen it happen so many times. An entrepreneur is faced with a problem, like collecting past-due accounts or motivating listless workers. But instead of rationally weighing all options, the entrepreneur jumps emotionally on the first solution that comes to mind. Angry that customers are taking too long to pay, the owner hires an expensive collection agency; fed up with employees, he or she fires the entire staff and starts over with new workers. Wise entrepreneurs, however, examine thoughtfully and carefully each problem they face, big or small.

Initial responses can be too irrational, too despairing. Relax, think clearly, and consider all the possibilities. Choosing the right option can mean the difference between finding your treasure and perishing in the rapids.

As you journey through the jungle of entrepreneurship, move around the traps and pitfalls if you can. Don't brave the rapids if you can find the treasure by avoiding them. But how do you know when to attack and when to hold back, when to be aggressive and when to be passive? Fortunately, I have a plan that may help you decide whether to jump the ravine or build a bridge.

Spectrum Thinking

I've met dozens of successful entrepreneurs who have turned potential problems into windows of opportunity. And I've developed a decision-making process that will help you do it, too. I call it *spectrum thinking*. Here's how it works:

1. *Identify the obstacle or problem clearly*. Don't let irrelevant or extraneous concerns distract you from solving it. Focus on the challenge until you can describe it in ten words or fewer.
2. *Note the two most obvious solutions*. These solutions usually lie at opposite ends of the option spectrum. These are the do-or-

die options, and they rarely provide you with the practical, workable solution that usually lies somewhere in the middle of the spectrum.

3. *Create some alternatives that cover the entire spectrum of possibilities*. One of these options should give you the best solution.

Remember Tom Sawyer? This young adventurer was often saddled with problems, like the time he had to whitewash the gate around his house. He could have handled this problem in two obvious ways: He could have painted the fence, or he could have refused to do the work. But then he either would have missed a great day of fishing or would have been punished later for not doing his chores. Neither of these options seemed to be the best solution to his problem.

So, Tom used his resourcefulness and creativity to come up with another option that lay somewhere in the middle of those two extremes. He cleverly convinced two friends that they would have the time of their lives whitewashing the gate for him! Not only did he go fishing, but he managed to stay out of trouble as well.

I know an entrepreneur who used the same technique to create a fantastic growth opportunity for his small business. He had been running a very successful tailoring shop in a small building across the street from a large shopping mall. Because he offered the only professional alteration service near the mall, most people who bought clothing across the street would come to him for alterations.

But although his business was sailing smoothly along, and although he was well equipped for his adventure, an unexpected problem arose. When he went to his landlord to sign another lease, he found that his rent had been nearly tripled.

The landlord, actually quite sympathetic, explained, "I'm sorry. But I've recently been offered triple what you're paying me. A very successful fast-food company wants to use your space, and unless you can match the offer, I simply can't afford to pass up this opportunity."

"You know I'm not able to pay more for a new lease," replied the dejected tailor. "Isn't there anything you can do for me?"

The landlord responded, "I enjoy doing business with you, but I have to do what is best for *my* business. I'm sorry."

The great Ross Ice Barrier suddenly thrust itself into the tailor's path. And like a good explorer, the tailor exercised resourcefulness, determination, and clear thinking. He used the spectrum-thinking process.

First, he identified the problem. He needed another space to keep his business. He didn't waste time blaming his landlord or the fast-food company for forcing him out. Attributing blame wouldn't help him save the business. Neither did he waste time worrying about a financial setback or, even worse, the loss of his business. That would have been unproductive, undirected energy. Instead, he evaluated the problem and streamlined his energy so that he could devote all his attention to meeting effectively the challenge before him.

Next, he identified the two obvious do-or-die options. One, he could give up on his business and go into another line of work. Two, he could become angry and spiteful and sue his landlord. But as is often the case, neither of the do-or-die options was a good alternative. Which would be better—resigning himself to defeat by giving up on his dreams or embroiling himself in a lengthy, expensive, and bitter court battle?

Instead of choosing either of these alternatives, the tailor, like the jungle explorer standing at the dangerous edge of a steep ravine, used his resourcefulness and determination to meet his challenge. *He created alternative options that covered the entire spectrum of possibilities*:

- *He looked for the nearest alternative space*, resolving to sign another lease and establish firmer relations with a new landlord.
- *He spoke with clothing-store managers* in the mall, looking for someone who might rent him space inside their store.
- *He inquired about the availability of space* in the mall if he decided to open his store there.
- *He asked his current landlord if he could lease space* in the parking lot to run his business out of a trailer.

The tailor created several opportunities for himself. And he eventually moved forward on his adventure by finding an acceptable storefront space two blocks away. Certainly, the greater distance between his shop and the mall would hurt his business. To compensate for this loss, he improved his relationships with the employees of the clothing stores in the mall so they would send more customers to him.

When faced with an obstacle, a problem, or a misfortune, turn it into a *challenge* with *spectrum thinking*. Here's a quick recap:

1. *Focus your problem so you can describe it in ten words or fewer*. Think clearly and don't be sidetracked by extraneous con-

cerns. If you can't summarize your problem in ten words, then you haven't focused properly.

2. *Establish the two obvious solutions—usually do-or-die options.* These are the ends of the option spectrum. These should be easy to come up with.

3. *Create at least four options between the two ends of the spectrum.* Be resourceful and persevere; there are always more options than those at either end. Chances are, one of these options will work well for you.

Professor Challenge

Believe me, this is one of the best things about your business venture: *Problems make the adventure challenging.* The most rewarding aspect is not finding the treasure but rather experiencing the adventure itself. Driving down the left lane of the autobahn in a Mercedes 450 SEL at 140 mph isn't thrilling because you get to the *biergarten* faster. The *speed* is the thrill! Getting there is half the fun. *The adventure is the treasure!*

I like to think of the problems, obstacles, and challenges I encounter as being *teachers*. Each time I encounter a barrier, each time I come across a pitfall or a trap, I learn from the experience. *Obstacles, hurdles, and pitfalls in the jungle of entrepreneurship are like teachers: they grab you by the collar, pull you into their classrooms, and teach you lessons.*

When you were in school, teachers didn't give you homework and tests because they meant to punish you or to fail you (although it often seemed like that). Teachers were there to help you, and the assignments they gave you were designed to improve you. Think the same of difficulties you encounter in business. Use the problems you face to improve yourself, to move forward, and to find success.

Expect to encounter obstacles on your adventure, and look forward to them. They can offer tremendous opportunities to improve your expedition. Think carefully about the problems you face, consider a variety of possible solutions, and pick the one that best suits you. Be resourceful. Persevere.

> *If you encounter water, build a raft;*
> *if you meet a ravine, raise a bridge;*
> *if you face a mountain, lace up your boots.*

But times do change and
move continuously.

Edmund Spenser (1552–1599)
Elizabethan poet

Imagine being on safari and plodding slowly through the heart of the African plains. You're two hundred miles and one week away from the nearest village. Everything you need to survive—food, water, cooking supplies, clothes, tents, and tools—is packed on the backs of your mules. Anything could be around the next thicket of trees. Anything might be across the next stream or on the other side of a grassy plain—a pack of lions on the prowl, a quicksand pit, a herd of charging elephants. A thousand hidden traps and pitfalls lay in front of you. Uncertainty and change are the only constants. The survival of your expedition depends on your ability to successfully meet change and avoid the snares.

I read about an elephant hunter who was trekking across a wide grassy plain. A herd of roaming zebra flanked one side and a distant forest the other. The sun sat high in the clear blue sky; a dull haze covered the horizon. The heat was suffocating; it hadn't rained in weeks. The hunter noticed the frantic rustling of small monkeys in the treetops and heard the sounds of their shrill cries pierce the air.

Because he was an alert traveler, he recognized this behavior as an advance sign of an impending rainstorm. If he hadn't noticed this warning sign, the storm could have come upon him suddenly and unexpectedly. The frightened mules would have scattered across the plain; supplies would have been ruined in the wind, lightning, and rain. The expedition, and possibly the lives of the expedition members, would have been lost.

But the hunter had his eyes and ears open. He recognized the signs and responded quickly. He led his team toward less treacherous terrain and instructed the native guides to secure the mules, safely store the supplies, and make camp in a nearby cave. Watching and listening for signs of change allowed him to save his expedition and to ensure that it would continue to run smoothly, efficiently, and productively.

To keep your business running smoothly and efficiently, you, too, must remain aware, especially in tracking the interests of your customers. *Consumer demands are like the weather on an African veldt: constantly, and often unexpectedly, changing.* Meeting the demands of your customers, keeping pace with the continual shifts in their wants and needs, requires constant, careful attention.

The Power of the Customer Perspective

Keep your eyes and ears open. Pay attention to customer interests, and let *them* determine the course of your expedition. Lao-tzu, a founder of Taoism, said, "To lead the people, walk behind them." *And the trick is leading people where they want to go.*

Several years ago in the Bordeaux region of France, I met a restaurateur who used this strategy and profited enormously. Every table was filled when we entered his small restaurant. He seated us within about five minutes and gave us menus. Every entrée looked excellent, so when the waiter approached I asked his opinion on the selection.

"Sir," he said, "I must say every dish is quite good, but the *risotto aux champignons* is the most popular. Almost every patron in here right now is eating that dish."

"Well," I said, "then I'll have the *risotto aux champignons*."

When my entrée arrived, the aromas alone stimulated my senses. After I had enjoyed the first bite of this Italian-style rice with mushrooms, I understood why the restaurant was packed. This dish was exceptional and the many regular customers loved it.

The owner visited our table, and I asked him how he developed this entrée. He had obviously been waiting for someone to ask him that question—he pulled up a chair and told me the story of the *risotto aux champignons*.

His secret to success, he said, was maintaining a constant stream of open communication with his customers. He spends much of his time walking from table to table, accepting compliments and, more important, soliciting feedback. What better way is there to find out what customers want than to ask them?

When he opened his restaurant six months earlier, he frequently posed as a customer to strike up a more candid conversation with a guest. Sitting in a booth one day, he casually asked a well-dressed couple at an adjacent table, "How is the risotto appetizer?"

"Oh, it's terrific," the woman promptly replied. "Try it—you'll love it. I just wish they served it as an entrée as well."

"Really?" the restaurateur asked.

"Oh, yes," her husband added. "It's excellent. The only problem is the small portion. We'd love to have it as a main course!"

The following evening, the waiters informed all the customers that the *risotto aux champignons* dish listed under the hors d'oeuvres section was also available as an entrée, by popular demand. When the owner ran out of mushrooms, he knew he had a winning dish. Since then, he said, the word spread, and many people have visited his restaurant just to sample the popular dish. I was impressed.

After dinner, as the restaurateur and I conversed about the challenge of running a small business, he added that he regularly sends a friend into his restaurant for dinner. The friend, acting as a normal customer, takes notes on the quality of food preparation and the service, and reports back to him. If the food is taking too long to come out of the kitchen or if the servers are not doing a good job of selling the dishes to the customers, adjustments are made. This entrepreneur understands the power of the *customer perspective* on his business.

Here is a summary of the simple techniques you can use to keep in close contact with your customers and to lead them where they want to go:

- *Have an in-depth conversation* with at least one customer every day.
- *Collect feedback* from your customers by pretending to be a customer in your own business (if possible).
- *Have a friend or business associate collect information* for you by assuming the role of a customer.

Study closely the wants and needs of your customers so you can anticipate their demands and respond to them *quickly*. A successful expedition must undergo constant revision and improvement in order to match constant change in the environment.

Use Your OARs

I have developed a method of watching and listening for signs of change. I call it OAR: Observe, Analyze, Respond. You can use this method on three planes.

The macro plane. The first plane is the large, macro plane. It involves looking at the big picture. Watch the overall business environment and choose your direction of travel according to the wants and needs of the community at large. Look for your niche in the jungle of entrepreneurship.

Michael Krasny used his OARs in a relatively simple situation and subsequently launched one of the largest mail-order computer vendors in the nation. He placed an ad in his local newspaper to sell his computer (he wanted some extra cash). When he received loads of calls, he realized he could have sold many computers. He *observed* a huge demand, quickly *analyzed* the potential market, and then *responded*, founding Computer Discount Warehouse in Northbrook, Illinois. The number of inquiries he received from the first newspaper ad doesn't compare to his volume today. In a recent month, Computer Discount Warehouse received more than 23,000 calls from customers eager to experience the company's competitive pricing and top-notch service!

On the macro plane, use your OARs to spot unoccupied niches in the marketplace. Find a big need and fill it!

The midrange plane. I call this the midrange plane because it involves using your OARs in a slightly smaller frame of reference. Bring your field of vision down a bit by tracking the general trends of your industry. If you own a clothing store, staying up-to-date on fashion trends is a must. If you build homes, you must know what styles are popular and which materials are the most practical and least expensive. Maintaining a strong bird's-eye view of your company's position in the marketplace will enable you to keep pace with the ever-changing needs of your customers.

Michael Fiorito used his OARs on the midrange plane to transform the messenger-service business in New York City. During the 1970s, messages were delivered by foot runners who raced through the city streets, wearing holes in the bottoms of their shoes. These runners could deliver documents to an office a few blocks away faster than the U.S. Postal Service could. But it's not difficult to imagine how even a well-conditioned runner could fall behind in the concrete jungle. The runners simply could not keep pace with the increasing demands of clients.

Fiorito *observed* the need for improvement within the industry and *analyzed* the situation. If he could get messages from one location to another faster than by foot, he could accomplish two things: he could increase the volume of his business by delivering more packages each day, and he could beat the competition by offering faster, better services.

He *responded* by creating one of the first messenger services in New York City to use bicycle, foot, *and* van services. If a customer needed paperwork delivered a few blocks away, Fiorito would send a bike messenger. If some sketches were needed across town, he would send a van. His company took off quickly. Originally run out of a basement in Manhattan, Early Bird Express Inc. is now a $7 million company with nine branches around the city.

But Fiorito didn't stop there. *Even after experiencing tremendous success, he continued to use his OARs.* When the emergence of fax machines threatened to cut into his business, he responded by creating a computerized network system that allows him to stay one step ahead of the competition.[1]

The micro plane. The third plane is the small, micro plane. Here, you apply the OAR method by focusing attention on the minor details of your business, such as phone-cord length and desk placement. Monitoring your business down to the smallest of details will allow you to maximize production and increase your profit margin.

Kaizen

Japanese businesspeople have a word that describes the idea of continual improvement: *kaizen*. The basic premise of *kaizen* is that everything can be improved—no part of a business operation ever reaches a state of perfection. This concept applies to all three planes: macro, midrange, and micro. From improving the reputation of your company in your industry to improving the placement of the tape dispenser on your desk, the process of continual improvement certainly will make your work life easier and may increase your profits significantly.

Championing *kaizen*, the Japanese ignore the old adage "If it ain't broke, don't fix it." Rather, they believe and put into practice the opposite: "If it ain't broke, fix it anyway."

Keep Your Feelers Out

Whether you respond to the internal needs of your operation or to the external demands of consumers and competing businesses, modification is always necessary. Through changes both big and very small, your business can always be improved.

Over the course of his many travels throughout Africa, Livingstone noticed how small changes in the temperature preceded significant shifts in the weather. This simple observation allowed him to make dramatic adjustments to his expedition. In the rainy season, this knowledge allowed him to predict possible travel delays. Further, when he noticed that temperatures were not rising as they should, he instructed his men to dig wells, which would usually fill with water within forty-eight hours.[2] Also, he could enforce water rationing so supplies would not be depleted. When the plains were dry and parched, Livingstone was able to save his expedition from certain disaster by *observing* the weather, *analyzing* the situation, and *responding*.

Captain James Cook took extraordinary precautions to protect his ship as he explored the Great Barrier Reef around Australia. His sailors observed that the ship was surrounded by a dangerous coral reef hidden just below the surface of the windswept waves. This desperate situation called for quick thinking. Cook responded by deploying several small boats around the main ship. These dinghies acted as feelers that relayed information about the location and height of the reef to the ship. Constantly analyzing the reports from the dinghies, Cook skillfully maneuvered his ship through the jagged reef and crashing waves.[3] He used his OARs when he needed them most, and his expedition proved an amazing success.

As you pilot your expedition through uncertain waters or over treacherous terrain, keep *your* feelers out. Stay alert—watch and listen for signs of change. The success of your business depends on constant attention and continual improvement.

> *As an entrepreneur, you are the captain of a ship heading upstream against the current. Use your OARs to maintain your speed and keep yourself headed toward the treasure.*

CHAPTER 15

Focus on Your Company, Not on Your Competitors

> *He that would govern others, first should be the master of himself.*
>
> Philip Massinger (1583–1640)
> English playwright

I'm sure you're familiar with this metaphor: business is warfare. The marketplace is a battleground on which competitors are pitted against each other in a struggle for survival. Each side designs and launches offensive and defensive campaigns. Each company studies the moves of the other in a high-stakes chess match called capitalistic combat. And it's winner take all. The company with the best product and the best marketing strategy rings the victory bell; the others are driven from the field—crushed.

Well, it's a nice analogy. Imagining that the jungle of entrepreneurship is teeming with similar adventurers all competing for the same treasure certainly can be advantageous. Thinking in these terms can help you foster the kind of assertive attitude it takes to succeed in the jungle. The problem with this mentality, however, is that it can lead to an overly aggressive approach to competition in the marketplace that is harmful to all parties involved in the battle.

The warfare analogy places too much emphasis on direct confrontation. If business is warfare, the analogy says, then the most successful company will be the most hostile and violent. It teaches entrepreneurs to roll up their sleeves and start throwing punches at the slightest hint of provocation. *But it isn't the best competitive strategy.*

Often, the threat of danger isn't even serious. The war cries of your competitors carry in the wind. What sounds close and intimidating is often just a lot of hot air. Livingstone recalled that on the African plains he heard the roars of lions loitering nearly two miles away. The sound, though terrifying, didn't represent a significant danger to Livingstone's party, for the lions were too far away to pose a threat.[1] Don't worry too much about the loud roar of the competition until you feel warm breath on the back of your neck!

Besides, even if the danger is real, you don't need to launch big offensive and defensive campaigns in response to your competitors' attacks. You don't always need to battle your enemies to be successful. My experiences in the jungle of entrepreneurship have taught me to avoid competitive battles and instead to focus on my business. *So when the competition gets tough, take care of your business!*

Don't get involved in a competitive battle with rival businesses! Becoming embroiled in a bitter, drawn-out conflict *won't help you.* Spending time, money, and energy in contention with other companies will not strengthen, improve, or expand your operation. But spending time, money, and energy on *your* company will help it remain successful.

Don't spend time worrying about your competition. Time spent thinking about your competitors' strategies is wasted time. You can do little, if anything, about your competitors and the way they run their businesses. They will always be working hard to improve their products, boost production, and devise new marketing strategies. And there's nothing you can do about that. Your time will be better spent toward growing your business.

Even if the nature of your business requires you to take on corporate giants, the best competitive strategy is still to focus on your company. That's the approach Snapple used to defend itself against an advertising blitz launched by Lipton and Nestea. Snapple found a niche in the ready-to-drink iced-tea industry by introducing a line of flavored teas, and the large corporations soon tried to muscle their way into Snapple's territory.

Snapple president, CEO, and co-founder Leonard Marsh opted to compete with Lipton and Nestea by directing Snapple advertising toward consumer needs. When Lipton launched what *Advertising Age* later called "a guerilla radio campaign" charging that Snapple makes its tea from reconstituted tea powder as opposed to Lipton's "real-brewed" product, Marsh did not counterattack. He could have answered the charges with vehement denials in magazine, radio, and television ads. Or he could have chosen to denigrate Lipton's products with equally malicious accusations.

Instead, Marsh focused attention on the strength of his products. Snapple's advertising agency developed television spots that featured letters from satisfied, excited Snapple customers. The campaign was a professional, strategic way to counter Lipton's accusations. The ads focused solely on the strength of the Snapple product and ignored Lipton's hostile criticisms.

The size and stature of the business or company you compete against are irrelevant. And the perceived threats of your opponent are irrelevant. Snapple's strategies worked—by the time of the *Advertising Age* article, Snapple controlled 37.1 percent of the ready-to-drink tea market, compared to Lipton's 26.4 percent and Nestea's 15.2 percent.[2] The lesson is clear:

Focus on selling your product, and don't waste money and energy attacking your competitors.

Security Needs

A quick review: Maslow theorized about a hierarchy of motives that determine human behavior, and he used a pyramid shape to diagram personal needs. At the base of the pyramid are basic physical needs, such as sustenance. After these needs are met, people pursue their next need on the hierarchy: safety.

On this level, people want to safeguard themselves from physical dangers. We want to secure protection from the weather, dangerous animals, attack by other people, and the like. Only after fulfilling the safety need can we pursue the higher-level needs: belongingness, esteem (to achieve and receive recognition), cognitive (to learn and understand), aesthetic (to find beauty), and self-actualization (to realize our potential).

The great explorers understood this principle well. Before Livingstone could focus on making discoveries (an esteem need), studying the language of a native village (a cognitive need), or finding a natural wonder (an aesthetic need), he had to secure himself from possible dangers of the terrain: droughts in the summer and vicious rainstorms in the winter, hungry predators, and tropical diseases. And Peary had to protect himself from the harsh polar climate before he could expend energy leading his expedition.

As an entrepreneur, you, too, must fulfill your safety needs before you can pursue the goals of monetary profits and personal satisfaction. You must know that your company is safe from attack so you can be a pragmatic, sensible leader of your expedition. You must establish for your company a certain feeling of security. Imagine that an adventurer scrambles up a tree to avoid a growling, hungry tiger. While he sits on a weak limb, fearful for his life, he doesn't take out his compass and rationally evaluate which direction his expedition should go the following day. In fact, he's probably pretty busy eyeing the wobbly branch and the hungry tiger below. Similarly, if you must continually worry about whether your company will be able to remain in business, you won't be able to focus on the two important elements of entrepreneurship: your company's growth and your enjoyment of the process.

The Fortification Technique

The best way to ward off competitors—to create security—is to focus on strengthening your business. You will reach a point when your company will appear so solid that nobody will try to take you on. I've developed a practical three-step process to help me create security for my businesses. I've used it with great success, and I'm confident you will find it helpful as well. By implementing these strategies, you'll fortify your business by building high, thick stone walls no competitor will be able to penetrate.

Create strong relationships with all your customers. You can build a powerful, sturdy base of operations for your business by establishing a firm clientele. If your customers are thrilled with your product and your service, and if, most important, *they really like you*, they won't leave to patronize a new competitor. Period.

Imagine you own a small grocery store. You have an excellent reputation around town for offering the freshest baked goods and the finest cuts of fish, beef, and poultry. Your store is also known for being well stocked and well maintained. The environment is warm, with soft jazz playing in the background. Your customers rarely stand in line to be checked out because you always keep plenty of registers open. Most important, you greet every customer who enters the store. You know many of their names because most of them live in the neighborhood. You've hired friendly employees who also develop personal relationships with the customers.

When an entrepreneur visits your store to examine the grocery business in your area and sees your interaction with your clients, he or she will be shocked and will go on to another neighborhood where the residents don't know the grocer personally. *Your strong hold on the customer base will prevent a competing company from stealing a portion of your business.* On the other hand, if you haven't established strong ties with your customers, your business is vulnerable to regular competitive challenges.

I recently witnessed a competitive battle that illustrates the point nicely. A prosperous and well-established bagel shop is on a corner on the route I take to my office. The owner opens around five o'clock each morning, and I frequently drop in a few minutes later for two hot raisin bagels and a cup of coffee—my breakfast on the way to the office. About six months ago, he was challenged by an upstart company that opened on the opposite corner. I'll call the established shop Manny's Bagels and the competitor Bagels Inc. (Names have been changed to protect the not-so-innocent.)

Manny's Bagels had been, from what I could tell, very profitable because it was the only bagel store in the area. But the coffee was sometimes stale, and the employees were often grouchy or just plain rude. I never knew what to expect when I visited Manny's because the quality of the food and service was so erratic.

Bagels Inc. took advantage of Manny's weaknesses to create a strong business. When it opened nearby, people in the neighborhood were eager to try it. *Because they had no strong affinities with Manny's Bagels, they were easily drawn away*. Bagels Inc. quickly built a regular clientele by focusing on more pleasant service and better products.

Create strong alliances with your suppliers. Your suppliers are the people who provide your company with the products you, in turn, use to please your customers. Because they have a direct impact on your customers' satisfaction with your business, your suppliers are a vital component of your entrepreneurial expedition. When they have a bad season, you have a bad season. If you don't get the best product from them, your customers don't get the best product from you. You can't run an efficient operation or offer quality goods and services without a strong supply chain. *Suppliers are the backbone of your company.*

You can strengthen your business by establishing firm, dependable relationships with your suppliers. Treat them fairly and respect them as entrepreneurs as well. Be especially careful in negotiating. Remember, they have to make a profit, too, and most important, they have to *feel good* about doing business with you. If you consistently negotiate them down to rock-bottom prices, they won't be too eager to do business with you.

Some of the best travelers and explorers had a keen sense of the importance of nurturing and sustaining suppliers. Livingstone, an excellent observer, noticed the inefficient methods some natives in South Africa used to gather food. When the fruit of a particular tree ripened, the natives would fell the tree to save themselves the trouble of climbing it to get the fruit. It was faster and easier to get the fruit by chopping down the tree. But it was easy only once because they had cut off their supply! They had quickly obtained a lot of fruit once, just as you may get a good deal from your supplier in one session of tough negotiating. But if you're not careful, you may be felling your tree while trying to get the fruit.

I know Manny's Bagels had trouble maintaining quality in its food products, and I would guess the reason is that Manny frequently cut down his fruit trees. Manny may have haggled with the food companies' sales reps to get rock-bottom prices and often threatened to switch to other suppliers for better prices. As a result, the companies that supplied him with coffee, flour, raisins, and poppy seeds had little desire to serve him well. They were making few if any profits from their business with him and he was unpleasant to talk to, so they had little motivation to deliver supplies on a regular, consistent basis. Because Manny negotiated such low prices, his coffee supplier probably mixed in bags of lesser-quality beans. The result? The quality of the store's coffee suffered, and customers were unhappy.

Or maybe Manny frequently carried through on his threats to switch suppliers, which resulted in frequent fluctuations in the quality of the store's coffee. His business oscillated with the quality of his products and the tenuous relations with his suppliers.

Mark Cohn was able to build Damark into a wildly successful, stable catalog company because he developed outstanding relations with the companies that supply him with products. He gets good deals, for sure, or his company wouldn't be able to sell their products (stereos, exercise equipment, televisions, computers, to name a few) for such low prices. But he has evidently nurtured his suppliers, allowing them to share in the success of his company. Cohn's strong alliances with the manufacturers benefit Damark, the suppliers, and most of all, Damark's customers.

Further, these relationships make Damark so solid that no companies want to infringe on his business. The start-ups can't even begin to compete with Damark's prices because they can't get the same good deals! *Cohn's excellent, long-standing relations with his suppliers prevent competitors from getting a foot in the door.*

Advertise the benefits of your business. Marketing strategies aimed at the detriment of your competitors succeed only in creating a climate of hostility. This kind of advertising will create competitive battles and lead to drawn-out campaigns—hurting rather than helping your profits.

Don't devise your marketing strategy around the weaknesses, defects, or shortcomings of your competitors. Advertise the benefits, strengths, and unique qualities of *your* business. Repetition breeds recognition. By frequently advertising the strengths of your company, you'll embed a positive image of your company in potential customers' minds and fortify your position in the market.

As your business is growing and you spot a flaw in your competitor's product or service, you'll be tempted to slander your rival. But this is like insulting another kid's bicycle on the playground. Perhaps you say that his handlebars are bent. Then the kid looks at your bike and says that your seat is crooked. Then the other kids gather around, watching you and the other kid throw insults at each other. Then punches start flying. And when the skirmish is over, the other kids walk away and one of them says, "I never realized Tommy's handlebars are bent." "Yeah," another chimes in, "and I never realized Billy's seat is crooked." The result of the battle is twofold: you have a bloody nose, and all the kids on the playground know the flaws of your bicycle, all because you couldn't be quiet about Tommy's handlebars.

Focus on *your* business. Fix up your bicycle—especially the crooked seat—so other kids don't have any reason to insult you. Then you can ride through the park without being disturbed.

Responding to Attack

Unfortunately, these strategies aren't totally foolproof. If a fool wants to take on your company, he or she will do it no matter how fortified you are. Sometimes a competitive battle is impossible to avoid. This is the nature of the free-enterprise system. Rival entrepreneurs may be wasting their time and money to attempt to wrest away from you a portion of the market, but that doesn't mean they won't try. As you become a skilled adventure entrepreneur, your share of the market will increase and you will make more and more money. When others see this, they will want to move in on your territory. This is a normal part of human nature.

Responding to a competitive attack is a difficult, delicate challenge, especially if your opponent is a larger, wealthier company. Your goal in the battle is simple: to end the conflict quickly with the fewest losses possible. Here are some dos and don'ts on handling encroachment by competitors.

Do defend your position. Defend your business by turning inward, as we've discussed. Strengthen your grip on the market by stepping up efforts to please your customers, maintain good relations with your suppliers, and advertise the benefits of your product or service.

But don't stop there. Don't be content to simply *hold* your position. *Advance!* The lives of Henry Morton Stanley and his crew, for example, depended on their ability to defend their position and repel the enemy. While traveling down the Congo River, Stanley's mere presence in the jungle incited the locals into a frenzy. When the natives attacked his boats, Stanley not only repelled them from his position on the river but also followed them into the forest. "We make straight for the banks and continue the fight . . . hunt them out into the woods, and there only sound the retreat, having returned the daring cannibals the compliment of a visit."[3] No doubt, defensive tactics such as this enabled Stanley to become the first man to successfully navigate a boat down the Congo to the sea.

As you pilot your expedition toward success, don't be content to repel the enemy; drive it all the way back to its camp.

Do use one powerful blow. *One of the big myths about competition in business is that you need to crush your opponents and drive them out of business.* This isn't necessarily true. You don't need to pound away at a weakened opponent to secure a strong hold on the market. Usually, one powerful blow is all it takes.

While traveling a westward route through China in the 1860s, Thomas Thornville Cooper encountered considerable hostility from the locals. At one point, he was attacked by a small group of bandits. In an effort to defend himself, Cooper fired his musket at the outlaws as a scare tactic. He wrote, "If a thunderbolt had fallen amongst the band it could not have created greater consternation." At that point, the bandits scattered into the hills unharmed, allowing Cooper to continue on his way.[4]

Cooper could have wounded or killed the bandits had he chosen to do so. But he remained content to frighten them with one powerful blow—a "thunderbolt." After all, there was plenty of room in China for Cooper and a few bandits to coexist without conflict.

The jungle of entrepreneurship is large enough to permit the peaceful coexistence of many businesses. Remember that your goal is to grow your company, not put somebody else out of business. When you become involved in a competitive battle, you don't have to keep firing until your opponent drops to the ground. One strong action by your company—a stunning development in customer service (thirty-minute pizza-delivery guarantee) or a new alliance with another company (Northwest Airlines and KLM)—will put your rivals on the run.

Don't create a long battle. Extended competitive battles are expensive, exhausting, and de-motivating. If you find yourself in a defensive position, don't plan for a drawn-out conflict. Act quickly and decisively to cease the skirmish.

Consider the competition between MCI and AT&T, two bitter rivals in the long-distance telephone-service business. For several years they have been attacking each another in print, radio, and television advertising. The effects of this drawn-out battle have been immense:

- *Monetary damage.* Each company spends vast amounts of money to keep pace with the marketing campaigns of the other. Each time MCI comes out with an ad or a commercial, AT&T must counter with a response, and vice versa. Both companies waste millions of dollars each year just to combat the other's strategy.

- *Consumer frustration*. A long battle can foster a deep sense of frustration and hostility among consumers. Customers tire of hearing companies berate and taunt each other. The negativity can, after a while, begin to trouble consumers who want to know more about the benefits they will receive from a company rather than the deficiencies they should avoid in another. Harsh campaigns like MCI versus AT&T can result in bad effects on the entire industry. If you own Pisa Pizza, for example, and you continually duke it out with your competitors, Pizzarama and Pizza House, area residents will become agitated. Eventually, they'll stop going out for pizza and will patronize the Mexican and Chinese restaurants instead.
- *Weaknesses revealed*. In drawn-out battles, the name-calling and accusations hurled by each company can become awfully vicious. In this kind of battle, you can be sure your opponent will discover and reveal each of your companies' weaknesses. And you will do the same to your competitors. From a utilitarian perspective, the battle is a waste of resources. Before the pizza competition, customers enjoyed the food at all three restaurants. After the battle, they're aware that all three pizza companies have deficiencies. The longer the battle continues, the more the customers will be aware of all three companies' shortcomings.

Don't become paralyzed. When your company falls under attack, the worst thing you can do is to become scared or paralyzed. In fact, you must be in control of your emotions and your senses, because fast, effective reaction can end the battle before it heats up.

Do not stand frightened. Instead, *make a vow of determination and meet the advance with your best defensive strategies.* Stanley recalled his thoughts just before being attacked by natives: "We have no time to pray, or to take sentimental looks at the savage world, or even to breathe a sad farewell to it. So many other things have to be done speedily and well."[5] With hundreds of spear-hurling natives bearing down on him, he had to act quickly.

Livingstone, too, recalled the necessity of acting quickly and keeping his wits about him when under attack. He described how an elephant, when stampeding through the jungle, can move very quickly. "His scream or trumpeting, when infuriated, will sometimes paralyze the horse that is unused to it; ... It not unfrequently happens that the poor creature's legs do their duty so badly that he falls and exposes his rider to be trodden into a mummy."[6] The only way to guard against this unfortunate experience is to prepare your horse ahead of time for such an unlikely event. *Expect to be challenged. And be prepared to act when it happens.* Plan your defensive strategies ahead of time. When you are rushed by a charging elephant, you'll be ready to defend yourself.

The best way to prepare for competition—whether a charging elephant or the rival bagel shop on the opposite corner—is to focus on *your* business. By strengthening and improving your business, you'll be able to avoid most competitive battles. If you are attacked, wage an intelligent, forceful, and short battle, and you'll come out on top.

You have only one set of eyes. Focus them on your company.

*Human felicity is produced
not so much by great
pieces of good fortune that
seldom happen, as by
little advantages that
occur every day.*

Benjamin Franklin (1706–1790)
American author, statesman, and scientist

Have you ever taken a moment over the course of a busy day to notice the magic of manipulating text on a computer? Or hesitated for a moment before answering the phone, thinking about how great it will be to talk with a prospective client? Have you paused while working to look outside and enjoy the beauty of the day, the joy of living? Have you ever really stopped, for just a moment, to notice the small, everyday occurrences that make your life so special?

There are a thousand little pleasurable events that take place over the course of the day—things that people often fail to notice or enjoy. There's that special moment as you walk into your place of business each morning when the still, quiet room waits for the day's business to begin. There is your pleasure when your employees joke with one another while they work, enjoying the time they spend working in your company, or when you watch a customer walking lazily through the aisles of your store, smiling, stopping to peruse the merchandise on the shelves.

These events occur every day! And they are all wonderful, all special. The small, simple details that together form the basis of daily activity in your business are among the most pleasurable events your venture adventure has to offer. These small occurrences, the seemingly trivial ones, are the things you have the opportunity to enjoy the most. *Too often, entrepreneurs have their sights focused so narrowly on the treasure that they fail to enjoy the details of the adventure—the minutiae that make the entire experience so fulfilling, pleasurable, and rewarding.*

Some of the world's greatest explorers have made the most of their adventures by taking time to find pleasure in the details. The Portuguese explorer Amerigo Vespucci (after whom the American continents were named) was famous in the sixteenth century for his incredibly detailed descriptions of his travels. He described with astonishing detail his first encounter with the New World. He and his crew sailed up the Amazon River and into Brazil. Notice Vespucci's attention to the specific features of the scene: "What I and my men saw there was an infinite number of birds of various forms and colors, and so many parrots, of such diverse kinds, that it was a marvel: some red . . . others green and red and lemon-yellow, still others solid green or black and flesh-colored." He described further "the delicate scents of the herbs and flowers, and the tastes of those fruits and roots."

Vespucci noticed every detail of the scene, although he had not yet reached his final destination. This spot was merely a viewpoint along the way. The spices, silks, gold, and silver he was seeking were still far down the trail.

Vespucci could have kept his eyes focused on the horizon, anticipating the end of his journey. He could have donned a pair of blinders to block from sight everything but the path before him. *Instead, he chose to take pleasure and satisfaction in the joy of the small things along the way.*

The best thing about Vespucci's travels was that each day brought with it more new land, another fantastic view. The same is true for your adventure. *Each new day will bring with it a host of new small experiences and a new array of pleasures.* Each day will bring more excitement, more vigor, more energy. And if you learn to appreciate the offerings of each day, you'll look forward to your adventure with more enthusiasm, more excitement, and more energy.

Columbus, one of Vespucci's contemporaries, captured the spirit of this idea as he sailed on his first voyage to America. He described the joy and the exhilaration with which he arose each morning by writing in his journal, "*Que era plazer grande el gusto de las mañanas*" ("What a delight was the savor of the mornings!")[1]

Each morning brought with it the beauty of the dawn: the image of a rose-colored sun, perhaps, sneaking behind clouds in the east as a gentle breeze lapped waves against the ships' hulls and filled the sails. Columbus looked forward to the start of each day partly because it brought him another step closer to his final destination and partly because it brought another glorious view.

Entrepreneurship is a wonderful, exciting adventure with a thousand little pleasures. As I conduct the day-to-day affairs of my business adventure, I find pleasure and fulfillment in the smallest of details, such as the following items I might enjoy in a typical five-minute period in my office:

- Sipping an icy root beer while I look over accounts
- Sitting in my comfortable desk chair

- Hearing a customer say "Thank you"
- Putting an envelope through the mailing meter, marveling at the speed of the machine
- Checking sales totals on the computer, awed by the efficiency of having a computer system at the core of the business
- Surveying an up-to-the-moment sales report
- Chewing two jelly beans from the bowl on my desk
- Watching an order spill out of the fax machine (I *really* enjoy that one!)

The small things prove to be the most exciting. Because I take so much enjoyment from the minor details, I leave my office each night feeling satisfied and fulfilled by the day's adventure.

Each day you walk into *your* office or store, remind yourself that the pleasure is in the journey, not in the destination. *If you don't look for the small pleasures, you won't find them!* If you come to the store or to the office every day without making a conscious effort to enjoy yourself, you probably won't. It's easy to become wrapped up in the monotonous drudgery of performing the same tasks over and over again each day.

Some of the best explorers occasionally fell into this mindset, hampering their enthusiasm and energy. While journeying to the North Pole, Peary remarked, "During the daily march my mind and body were too busy with the problem of covering as many miles of distance as possible to permit me to enjoy the beauty of the frozen wilderness through which we tramped."[2] A picturesque landscape of frozen ice stretched in every direction, but Peary didn't stop to enjoy it because he was too consumed with the drudgery of "covering as many miles" as possible.

Fortunately, the difference between the toil of covering more and more miles and the pleasure of enjoying the view is a *choice*. You can choose to look for the small pleasures along the way, or you can choose to be consumed in the monotony of your daily tasks. You can keep your eyes focused on the rear ends of your sled dogs, or you can look up to admire the view. *The choice is yours*. Your business adventure is filled with wonderful, exciting little pleasures, so why not choose to enjoy them?

Find Pleasure in the Commonplace

A U.S. surveyor and explorer who traveled west of the Rocky Mountains in the mid-1800s found a great deal of satisfaction in what seemed to be the most ordinary occurrences. During one journey in northern California, John

Charles Fremont described the approaching rain clouds that he and his men viewed from atop a low mountain: "Shortly . . . we heard the roll of thunder and, looking towards the valley, found it all enveloped in a thunderstorm. For us . . . it had a singular charm; and we watched its progress with excited feelings until nearly sunset."[3] Fremont and his company were traveling in the waning weeks of winter, just as spring was beginning to make itself felt. The view of approaching storm clouds couldn't have been an especially noteworthy occurrence—at that time of year, storm clouds were probably rolling through the mountains daily. But still, he and his men stopped to admire the "singular charm" of that storm for as long as daylight permitted. Fremont distinguished himself as an explorer by surveying and mapping a significant amount of land west of the Rockies, but *it was his ability to find pleasure in the commonplace events of his travels that brought smiles to his face.*

You may very well find fame and fortune on your adventure as well. And let's hope you do! But you can increase your happiness along the way by looking, as Fremont did, for the "singular charm" of common, everyday events. You don't have to wait until the big payoff at the end, the unearthing of the treasure, to allow yourself to be happy. Take pleasure in just a few of the thousands of wonderful things that happen each day! If you do, you'll find that the adventure itself is the big payoff.

Learn to Find Pleasure in the Defects

Not only do explorers pay attention to the wonderful little details, but some find ways to turn small irritations into small delights. Évariste Régis Huc, a nineteenth-century French missionary traveling through China toward Tibet, described the simple experience of assembling a caravan and preparing for departure.

> The plaintive cries of the camels, the grunting of the yaks, the neighs of the horses, the shouts and the noisy songs of the travellers, the thin whistles with which the lakto urged on the baggage animals, and above all the innumerable bells hanging from the necks of yaks and camels—all these produced an immense, indescribable concert, which far from being fatiguing, appeared on the contrary to inspire everyone with courage and energy.[4]

Can you imagine rising early in the morning and preparing for a lengthy, arduous day of traveling while the grunts and snorts of pack animals and the obnoxious roar of the crowd echo in your ears? Huc could have moaned and complained about the ruckus. He could have become angry and grouchy. *Instead, he drew "courage and energy" from this chorus of sounds. He took pleasure in this "concert" of noises.*

You'll be a happier and more successful entrepreneur if you learn to take pleasure in the noises that occasionally intrude on your business. Many times, you can view the small irritations as small signs of success. For instance, the roar of laughter and carrying on you hear in the back room of your store isn't just a sign that work has stopped. Perhaps it has momentarily, but think of it as an indication of good employee morale in your company. Be pleased that your workers enjoy themselves on the job, for they are likely to be more productive if they are happy.

Celebrate Small Victories

One good way to take pleasure from the simple things is to celebrate your small victories. *Don't just enjoy them, celebrate them.* You can do this frequently; two or three times a day will help you stop and take note. This strategy will help you place more emphasis on the adventure rather than on the treasure.

For example, if a large order comes in, I might enjoy a few jelly beans from the jar on my desk. When a satisfied customer asks to speak to me to thank me for my company's good service (which happens about every other day), I applaud myself by taking a five-minute break to go outside and savor the sunshine.

There are a hundred small things you can do to celebrate. You don't have to throw a huge party every time you get a new client or uncork the champagne every time you have a strong day of sales. But you can have small celebrations to remind yourself that small achievements are important, too. Don't just sit back and convince yourself that you do enjoy the small experiences of your life. *Celebrate the numerous victories you experience every day!*

The Myth of Timbuktu

Most people look forward only to the big accomplishments in business: large receipts at the end of the day, landing a big account with a new client, breaking a record for annual sales, or opening a new location. They think the treasure is the reward. *But this view is a narrow and erroneous perspective on the venture adventure.*

By focusing only on the treasure—the amount of money you plan to make—you not only prevent yourself from enjoying the small details of your adventure, but you set yourself up for possible disappointment. When you place large expectations on that one final triumph, the one gigantic pay-off, you attach a significance to it that can never be matched by the reality of the treasure.

Building up unrealistic expectations of the treasure was a problem for many famous explorers. Many Europeans placed high hopes on the fabled African city of Timbuktu. For more than three hundred years, fabulous rumors of Timbuktu's incredibly wealthy market circulated throughout Europe. Tales of the city's wealth were legendary: gold, silver, spices, and handmade crafts were said to flow through its market like water through Venice.

But traveling to Timbuktu was nearly impossible. Located on the southern tip of the great Sahara Desert and on the banks of the Niger River, the city was forbidden to all but the Muslims of Africa and Arabia. To get there, Europeans had to brave a perilous journey: traveling the rugged land from the west coast of Africa, battling bandits along the way, fighting disease-infested swamps and quagmires, and negotiating with the hostile natives. For more than three hundred years, explorers attempted the journey. But none succeeded in reaching the city.

Finally, in 1827, René Caillé, a French explorer, reached Timbuktu and returned safely. You can imagine the high expectations Caillé and the rest of Europe had for the discovery of this fabled city: A new source of practically unlimited wealth would finally be available to the Western world. But Caillé's observations fell far short of his expectations:

> I looked around and found that the sight before me did not answer my expectations. The city presented . . . nothing but a mass of ill-looking houses built of earth. Nothing was to be seen in all directions but immense plains of quicksand of a yellowish white color. The sky was a pale red as far as the horizon; all nature wore a dreary aspect, and the most profound silence prevailed.[5]

Timbuktu lay in dilapidated decay; its glorious market had ceased to exist centuries earlier. Talk about disappointment! What was imagined to be Timbuktu's wealth and glamour was in reality a mere shadow of what had existed centuries ago.

The point here is not that the treasure you seek will probably disappoint you. Not at all. In fact, money can enrich your life and the lives of those close to you. The message is this: Pay attention to the small pleasures you can experience in the everyday activities of running your business. If you can learn to take pleasure in the minute details, you'll have fun along the way, and you'll more than likely be pleased by the success you experience, regardless of the size.

Stay Alert

Keep in mind, however, that taking time to enjoy the small, pleasurable activities of day-to-day business can be extremely rewarding—and distracting. Take care not to lose sight of your primary responsibility—making profits. Only with profits can you pay your employees, buy supplies, and grow your operation. *Don't allow admiration for the small details of the scenery along the way to distract you from seeking profitability.*

Allowing pleasures and delights to steal your attention from the immediate task at hand can prove to be a dangerous, costly mistake. One nineteenth-century explorer, Paul du Chaillu, nearly paid a heavy price for drifting away in an enchanted reverie. The Frenchman, traveling through a North African forest, explained how

> far away in the east loomed the blue tops of the farthest range of the Sierra del Crystal, and, as I strained my eyes toward those distant mountains which I hoped to reach . . . I dreamed of forests giving way to plantations, . . . of peaceful [natives], . . . of churches and schools; and, luckily raising my eyes . . . saw pendent from the branch of a tree beneath which I was sitting an immense serpent, evidently preparing to gobble up this dreaming intruder on his domains.[6]

Admiring a vision of the landscape caused Chaillu to forget that he was on a dangerous adventure, a journey marred by many obstacles and hidden pitfalls. And it nearly cost him his life. Enjoy the beauty of the adventure, but remain aware that you are on an adventure and that problems which demand immediate attention arise constantly.

Capturing the spirit of adventure entrepreneurship involves taking pleasure in the adventure itself. Explorers didn't spend years away from their families and risk their lives just to return with riches; they explored because they savored the adventure. Finding your treasure undoubtedly will be a joyous experience, but your true satisfaction and fulfillment will come from your perceptions of the journey. Samuel Taylor Coleridge, the nineteenth-century English poet, understood this insight. He wrote, "The happiness of life is made up of minute fractions—the little soon forgotten charities of a kiss or smile, a kind look, a heartfelt compliment, and the countless infinitesimals of pleasurable and genial feeling."

Wait not for the awesome view from the top of the mountain. Savor the glorious smells, sights, and sounds on the way up.

Take calculated risks.
That is quite different
from being rash.

George S. Patton (1885–1945)
United States Army general

Most people think of entrepreneurs as risktakers, daredevils, or crazy gamblers who flirt not with physical danger but with financial ruin. Reckless abandon seems to define their careers. Security is an unwanted luxury; rationale is a vague abstraction; caution is an afterthought. Entrepreneurs stake themselves, and their money, on half-baked schemes that promise either bankruptcy or wealth. Most people think of business as a risky adventure and of entrepreneurs as willing travelers in search of pay-dirt on uncertain, danger-ridden courses.

Scott Schmidt, though, is certainly no risktaker. This modern-day adventurer pioneered the popular modern sport of extreme skiing, which involves the performance of daredevil stunts. Schmidt makes an excellent living skiing over sixty-foot cliffs, because several companies produce and sell videos of his jumps. *Business Week* reported that Schmidt "appears a reckless maniac," though "for every jump, he has carefully charted the take-off point and landing." He knows ahead of time what is going to happen—how he will jump and where he will land—and then he trusts his talent and ability as a skier to pull him through. Schmidt is no madman. Each stunt is carefully, deliberately planned. He leaves nothing to chance.[1]

The perception of entrepreneurs as lunatic daredevils is false one. Business is not a blackjack-like gamble, and entrepreneurs are not gamblers. Gamblers abandon all control and submit to the demon Chance. They roll the dice and hope their numbers will come up. Luck is the final arbiter of their fortunes: they may win big, or they may lose everything. Either way, rolling the dice is an act of random uncertainty. Gamblers have no way of knowing what will happen.

Being an entrepreneur is like playing with loaded dice: you know what the outcome of the roll will be. An entrepreneur researches the industry, performs tests, and learns about the market. The demons Chance and

Luck are held at bay by the entrepreneur's knowledge, skill, and training in the field. As an entrepreneur, *you* control what kind of business you will operate, how much money to invest in it, where to build it, and how to put it all together. *You* have control.

Yes, entrepreneurs take risks. *But they are calculated risks.* Entrepreneurs invest time, money, and energy in business only after completing a process of evaluation. Before taking the first step, the entire journey is studied from all angles. A rough estimate of the outcome is predicted. Yes, risk is involved. But the risk is minimized substantially. Ventures without promise are avoided. *Entrepreneurs take risks because they know they will succeed.*

A Purdue University study cited in *Business Week* indicated that the vast majority of entrepreneurs are not risktakers. In fact, it's just the opposite. The number-one reason people decide to go into business for themselves is so they can use their skills. Cited as the number-two motivation is the desire to gain control over their lives. Fewer than 20 percent interviewed claimed they started their businesses solely for the potential of making money.[2] *Most people who start businesses aren't daredevils looking for big thrills and big prizes.* They're people, many of them conservative and all of them rational and thoughtful, who want to put their skills to the best use and gain control over their lives. Monetary profits, then, are simply further benefits of an already fulfilling lifestyle.

The Coffee-Store Gamble

If an entrepreneur doesn't perform a careful evaluation of the risks involved in a venture, the business then becomes a gamble. *Rushing blindly into your venture adventure is like rolling the dice with hope as your only preparation—you may win, but you may not.* If you don't study carefully the jump you are about to make, if you don't map out exactly where you will take off and where you will land, you may soon find yourself gripping the side of a mountain, hanging on for dear life!

Recently, a couple opened a small coffee store not too far from my office. They chose a location in a strip mall about half a block away from the corner of a fairly busy intersection. The mall had several tenants who had remained for many years: a spaghetti restaurant, stock-brokerage office, print shop, travel agency, and diving-supplies store. (Don't ask me how a diving-supplies store makes any money in Arizona—maybe they know something I don't.) But I'd also seen quite a few businesses come and go in that mall over the years: a bookstore, sandwich shop, women's golf store, hair salon, and several others I can't remember. The mall housed some successful businesses, but it didn't have a great track record for tenant longevity. So I was curious why the couple chose this mall for their coffee venture.

After the store had been open for a couple of days, I decided to pay them a visit, just to meet the new entrepreneurs on the block. When I walked into the store, I was very impressed. Attractive wood tables and chairs were arranged neatly in a well-kept room; there was an interesting display of eclectic artwork; a faint sound of easy jazz emanated from small speakers attached to the walls; the aromatic smell of fresh Columbian Dark Roast filled the air. The whole atmosphere was very pleasant, very relaxing, and very quaint—just what a good coffee store should be.

But what really impressed me was the couple who owned and operated the store. They were charming and very enthusiastic about their business. *I could tell instantly that they had the spirit of adventure entrepreneurship.* They were excited to finally be in control of their destinies.

As I walked to the counter, the woman greeted me with a warm smile and said, "Good morning! It's nice to see you today. How can I help you?"

I said hello and told her that all I really wanted was a cup of coffee.

Waving her hand across the counter, she beamed at me and explained, "We have four coffees brewed, which you can have by the cup. We also have thirty-five other coffees you can purchase by the half-pound or pound to brew at home." She told me about all the varieties that lay in the bins beneath the display case. And I'm sure she would have explained to me the taste and history of each coffee bean had I not broken in and ordered a cup.

That's when her husband spoke. "We'd love to give you a half-pound of ground coffee to take home as our gift," he said. "You can sample it and share it with your family."

I could see that he was excited about his product, he was eager to have people try it, and most important, he understood the *power of samples.* I paid for my cup of coffee and chose a Decaf French Roast to take home, then stood for a few moments chatting with them about their new business.

As I was leaving, I thought that these two people had everything going for them. They had a nice store, knowledge of their product, and were a novelty in the area; no nearby competition existed. Even more important, they were excited about their business, were very friendly and accommodating, and had studied the best marketing tactics for the coffee business. They had done everything correctly, except that they had forgotten to . . . *calculate the risk!* I noted that no other customers had come into the store while I was there. When I scanned the parking lot, I noticed that it was nearly vacant. A couple of cars were parked in front of the stock brokerage and a few in front of the print shop. There simply was not enough traffic in the mall. People would be most likely to stop in for a cup of coffee if they had other things to do in the mall, but few would pull into the mall just to buy a cup of coffee or a bag of beans. This couple had put their entire savings into their business. And I knew immediately that they would never make it, because they wouldn't do enough volume to break even.

In fewer than three months, the coffee store was gone. A simple analysis of realities—an easy calculation—would have told anyone that a coffee store in that mall was a bad idea. The couple could have easily predicted what would happen to their business in that location and could have chosen a storefront with more walk-by traffic. Instead, they launched their expedition without calculating the risk, and they were roasted.

The Risk Calculation

I figure it this way. The couple used about $12,000 cash in startup costs (the bare minimum for a retail business), which included things like tables, chairs, coffee grinders, counters, a cash register, lighting fixtures, and art. The store would require about $1,000 per month to pay monthly bills: $600 for rent (also the bare minimum), $250 for utilities, and $150 for advertisements and supplies.

Let's say that the couple wanted to recover their startup costs in one year—an ambitious goal for a large restaurant, but not for a small store. This means they had to make $2,000 per month for the first twelve months of the business: $1,000 to cover monthly fixed costs plus a one-month fraction of the startup costs ($1,000). That is, using a thirty-day month, they had to make about $67 per day just to break even at the end of the year.

Now, I know they sold a regular cup of coffee for $1.20. The coffee and the cup probably cost them twenty cents, so they were making about $1 on each cup of coffee. They would have to sell sixty-seven cups of coffee per day to *break even*—about six or seven cups an hour if they are open ten hours a day.

But to make things worse, when I walked into the coffee shop the next week, I saw an employee working for them. If the employee was working full time for minimum wage (with regular benefits), that's roughly $12,000 a year, or another $1,000 per month. The couple would have to sell an additional thirty cups of coffee per day, or a total of nearly one hundred cups every day, to cover their costs.

There is no way the mall could support that volume of business. But just for the sake of argument, let's say a spaceship crash-landed in the parking lot in front of their store, tourists from around the world flocked to the spot, and the couple sold two hundred cups of coffee per day—double what they need to break even. At that pace they would make roughly $36,000 per year in profits, assuming they were open every day of the year. The numbers just don't make sense. Two people earning $36,000 jointly means that each of the two entrepreneurs is taking home $18,000—and that's only if aliens land in the parking lot! The potential return isn't high enough to justify the risk.

Testing Your Ideas

If the nice couple had performed a few simple tests, they would have determined quickly that the location in the strip mall was not the ideal spot for their business. If they had spent a few hours at another successful coffee store, they would have figured out how much traffic they could expect in a good location. And if they had simply sat in the parking lot of the mall for two days (maybe a Friday and a Saturday) counting and observing the flow of people, they would have realized that there wouldn't be enough traffic to support their store.

Simple tests help you calculate the risk for any action, whether major, like starting a business, or relatively minor, like advertising your current business in a magazine. There are many ways to check the waters or examine the weather before you dive in or set sail. Many entrepreneurs use the following tests to calculate the risk of their ventures. And they should prove useful to you as well. *Before I embark on any new venture adventure or pursue a new direction in my current companies, I use these tests to assess the riskiness of my action.* From a statistician's perspective, they are rather inaccurate. But these tests are quick and easy, and they haven't failed me yet.

Phone surveys. I call people and ask them questions about their interest in the goods or services I plan to offer. You can gather great insight into consumer interests by simply calling people and talking to them.

I frequently use the random phone-survey test to collect instant feedback on a business idea. Recently I drove by an auto-repair shop and saw a large sign that said something like ENGINE STEAM-CLEANING ONLY $35. CLEAN OUT OIL AND GRIME! MAKE YOUR ENGINE RUN LONGER! Because I'm not a car buff, I hadn't heard of engine steam-cleaning. But the idea was interesting, so I stopped in. The mechanic was in the process of steam-cleaning one car, and two waited to be serviced. I talked to the two people who sat in the shop, waiting to have their engines cleaned.

"What is steam-cleaning, actually?" I asked.

One obviously didn't feel like talking. He adjusted his Chevy baseball cap on his head and opened a magazine. The other guy answered.

"They just take a steam machine and push the nozzle into all the nooks and crannies in the engine compartment. They get all the grime off, so the engine looks new again."

"So you pay for this just so your engine looks new again?"

"Actually, having the engine steam-cleaned is supposed to make it last a lot longer."

Mr. Chevy Cap became interested. "Yeah," he chimed in, "it's better to have a clean engine. The only thing I don't like is waiting around here to have it done."

So I paid to have my engine steam-cleaned, and I watched the mechanic do it. The process wasn't too complicated, and the machine didn't look especially expensive. While he was cleaning, I was thinking, "Would car owners like to have this service done at their homes? I could equip vans with the steam-cleaning machine pretty easily."

But I didn't know whether people would be willing to pay for such a service. I didn't know what kinds of people would want the service—the demographics of my potential customers. So I called local residents and asked some questions.

My technique wasn't statistically accurate, but it worked. I picked random phone numbers from the telephone directory. I said, "I'm an entrepreneur, and I live here in the city. I'm considering starting a business, and I would be very appreciative if you could give me a little feedback. My idea is to offer engine steam-cleaning services at people's homes. The steam-cleaning process removes all the dirt, oil, and grime from all the parts under your hood—making the engine look brand-new again. Also, many people believe steam-cleaning makes the engine last longer. Would this kind of service appeal to you?"

After finding out if they wanted the service, I asked them how much they would be willing to pay. When people were convinced that I wasn't a salesman in disguise, they gave me some honest replies. Many people ended the conversation by saying something like, "Good luck, and when you do get the business started, I'd love to have my engine steam-cleaned!"

By spending just a few hours on the phone, I gathered a wealth of information on my business idea. I never launched this business because . . . well, frankly, running three growing companies at once is enough of a challenge for the time being. I think there's a great opportunity here, though, and if you jump on it, my feelings won't be hurt.

Knocking on doors. This is another good way to gather information from consumers. As an alternative to phone surveys, this method of testing consumer interest allows you to get more direct feedback from potential customers. If you plan a local business, you can target the areas in which most of your potential customers live. Plan a list of questions that will help you collect the information you need, and start knocking on doors!

Talking to other business owners. If you need to know more information about potential startup costs for your business, or if you want to find out what normal fixed costs are in the industry, you can talk to other business owners. *Generally, entrepreneurs who own and operate businesses enjoy what they do and are eager to talk about their experiences.*

Sometimes, business owners will be a little apprehensive about your questioning if they sense you are a possible competitor. Some entrepreneurs I know call or visit business owners in other cities. If you are opening a bagel shop in Dallas, you might call the owner of a bagel shop in Boston to ask some questions. The established business owner shouldn't feel threatened if you're planning a store several thousand miles away.

Direct mail. This method works well if you plan to launch a company that will operate on a scale larger than a local or citywide business. Direct mail involves sending advertisements, questionnaires, and surveys through the mail, and it will allow you to reach a much wider audience.

If you are launching a public-relations firm specializing in representing, say, charitable foundations, you might mail surveys to the directors of one thousand small foundations in the United States. Remember, though, that average returns for any kind of direct-mail piece are in the 0.5 percent to 2 percent range, so you'll probably get back between five and twenty responses to your survey. If you'd like to receive one hundred responses, you'll have to send out ten thousand or more surveys. Although direct mail can be an accurate, comprehensive testing technique, it is also one of the more expensive ways to gather input on a business idea.

Starting your business is an adventure, but it is a deliberate, carefully planned adventure. Of course, there is risk involved. There will always be a certain element of risk in a business venture. But after all, isn't that what makes entrepreneurship so exciting?

Pierre Corneille, a seventeenth-century playwright, wrote, "To win without risk is to triumph without glory." Risk is paramount to the success of your business; without it, there is no joy, no thrill, and no eminence. But the risk in starting a business is not the equivalent of a foolhardy game of chance. Prepare well for your adventure, plan carefully the course you will take, and test the waters before you set sail.

Gamblers put their money on the pass line because they feel a 7 or 11 coming up. Entrepreneurs put their money on the pass line because they know there is a 4 out of 21 probability of rolling a 7 or 11. Both take risks. Only one has a calculated prediction of the outcome of the roll.

> ***Before you leap across the entrepreneurial gorge,***
> ***calibrate the distance of your running start, your take-off point,***
> ***and your launch speed and angle to be certain you won't***
> ***land a few feet short of the cliff on the other side.***

*The greater thing in this
world is not so much where
we stand as in what direction
we are going.*

Oliver Wendell Holmes (1809–1894)
American physician, author, and speaker

Marshall E. Dimock has some sage advice that applies particularly well
to entrepreneurs. The author of *A Philosophy of Administration Toward
Creative Growth*, he says, "Fixing your objective is like identifying the North
Star—you sight your compass on it and then use it as the means of getting
back on track when you tend to stray."[1] Your North Star is your vision of an
ideal lifestyle. Later in this book, we'll examine the concept of vision.

*After you've identified your North Star, you can use it as a guidepost
by which to judge the progress of your journey.* If you veer off on a side
path, use it to keep yourself from getting lost in the wilderness.

*As you journey along on your adventure, you'll find that you can't
always plan what path to take, but you should always know where you're
going.* Before you begin your adventure, fix solidly in your mind a clear,
definitive objective—a specific destination. Begin the adventure by heading
toward that goal, but be open to possible alternative routes. Sometimes
a more roundabout trail will suit your purposes better than a direct path—
as long as you know where you're going, what you're doing, and why you're
doing it.

Effective Detours

When you do depart from the main trail, be aware that you are doing so
and take care not to lose sight of your destination. Often, entrepreneurs
stumble around in the woods simply because they've lost sight of their destinations. They wander, following the sound of the wind, going through the
motions, with no clear sense of purpose. They veer off on one side path
after another without stopping to orient themselves, and before too long
their final objective is either a vague and distant memory or a treasure too
far removed from the present expedition to ever be recovered.

You must be aware of your current location at all times. You won't be able to decide what route to take next if you aren't fully cognizant of your current position. If you don't know where you are, there is no way to determine in what direction to head to reach where you want to be! Consult your compass frequently to monitor the progress of your business adventure.

In the jungle of entrepreneurship, large obstacles will prevent you from traveling in a straight path, and you may be forced to go east or west to avoid them. When a mountain, a wide canyon, or a swamp impedes your trail, the most efficient strategy will be to circumvent the obstacle by taking a detour. Occasionally, you'll *choose* to depart from the main course, but many more times you'll be *forced* to do so.

Perhaps you'll be forced by your need for a stronger cash flow to branch into subsidiary areas. You might discover that to keep pace with the competition, your startup cola company will have to branch out into flavored and sparkling waters. But even when you opt to lead your expedition on a detour, do not lose sight of your main objective. *Consult your compass frequently. Use it to monitor your progress in the journey to reach your North Star.*

Tools of the Trade

Early explorers had crude methods of plotting their courses of direction. The compass was the primary tool, but they also used charts, mathematical tables, astronomy, and geometry. Finding the way was possible, but it involved more guesswork and approximation than precise analysis. Desmond Wilcox, in his excellent book on exploration titled *Ten Who Dared*, describes the inaccurate methods used by the early explorers who sought a westward passage to the Indies. He writes that, for those navigators,

> determining longitude was still impossible, but one could navigate crudely with a combination of instruments and dead reckoning, a chancy technique that combined deductions with guesswork. Ships ran north or south to a latitude line and then followed the line. The route to the Indies, went the saying, was "south till the butter melts, then due west."[2]

Guesswork and rough estimates guided the travels of the world's earliest explorers. Fortunately, you do not have to use those kinds of crude tools in combination with guesswork. You have much more advanced technology to help you check your progress and orient yourself toward your goals.

You don't have to travel "south till the butter melts"! Business is easy to gauge, and as an entrepreneur, you have a tremendous variety of tools that can help you accurately plot the progress of your expedition. Numerous books, manuals, consumer reports, surveys, and polls on every industry can provide you with specific, focused information. Many successful entrepreneurs share information in seminars, at conventions, on television, and on audiotapes.

However, *numbers are the compass of business—you judge the progress and location of your company by examining sales and income figures.* You can process data to monitor your market share, advertising spending, periodic sales, and other indicative numbers. Use this information frequently to help you locate your business in relation to your final destination.

I use my compass—an advanced sales-analysis program on my computer—every day to monitor company development. And so do other successful entrepreneurs. *In fact, most entrepreneurs perform an almost continuous process of reevaluation—they constantly monitor their markets to be sure they are heading down the most promising path.*

Changing Directions

Bob and Cindy Maynard, the owners of Country Walkers Inc., redirected the course of their business down the path of greatest profitability in both monetary and personal terms. In fact, the Waterbury, Vermont-based couple decided they were headed entirely in the wrong direction, so after twelve years of running Vermont Country Cycling Inc., a successful bicycle-tour company, they consulted their compass and decided that the bicycling business was no longer taking them toward their North Star. They reversed course and started a travel company that orchestrates walking tours all over the world. They literally walked off in a new direction! (There is some strong symbolism in this story.)

In a recent conversation, Cindy told me, "The bicycling business really got too big. It seemed like it was running us, rather than us running it. So we scaled back to a smaller business."

But the Maynards didn't exactly drop one expedition in favor of another. Their experience arranging cycling tours provided them with plenty of experience for the new business. Cindy explained, "It wasn't like we were getting into something we knew nothing about. We run essentially the same business. We know how to provide tour services, and we still market the business in the same way. We still offer the same basic product." As a reward for their skillful navigating, the Maynards exceeded $500,000 in sales after only two years in Country Walkers Inc., their new business.[3]

Venturing off on a side course, however, will not always prove to be a profitable experience. Columbus, who always kept his original goal (a westward route to the Indies) as his number-one priority, knew the advantages of heading down an alternate path as well as the disadvantages of not returning to the main route.

Uncertain of what to expect on their first voyage, Columbus and his crew were constantly scanning the horizon in hopes of finding an island that could serve as a resting point. On one particularly tranquil afternoon, after more than ten days at sea, a crewman on the *Pinta* rejoiced in shouting "Land ho!" as he spotted an island. A devout Catholic, Columbus sank to the floor in prayer and ordered that the crew sing *Gloria in Excelsis Deo*. The appearance of land seemed a sign of God's grace, and the entire crew, Columbus included, eagerly anticipated the forthcoming landing.

Columbus veered from his course and headed toward the island. The next day, however, brought no sight of land. Columbus concluded that a cloud bank hovering just above the sea must have given the illusion of land where none existed. Some crew members still believed they had seen an island and wanted to stay on the alternate path. But Columbus resisted their urgings because he knew that his object was to reach the Indies, and he thought that it would not make sense to delay.[4]

Columbus thought that the island presented an opportunity for his expedition, even though it was slightly off course, so he altered his direction. But as soon as the detour proved unprofitable, he quickly regained his original course.

The Life Adventure

What's so interesting about the Maynards' story is that their shift in *business* translated into a shift in their *lives*. Said Cindy of the transition, "It was more of a lifestyle change than anything else." *They modified their business adventure because they wanted to make a significant change in the course of their lives.* Their work with their business compass resulted in a change in their life's direction.

The orienting strategy you've learned in this chapter is applicable not just to your venture adventure but to your life as well. The decision to become an entrepreneur is an exciting one, and it often entails a big transformation in lifestyle.

Many people simply float through life with no clear sense of direction or purpose. They are borne along by the currents and don't exert much energy in one direction or another; they slump passively in tiny rafts and allow life to push them here or there.

It's easier to drift through life without thinking much about where you're headed and how you're going to get there, but it's a lethargic and unsatisfying way to live. It's like being the twelfth player on a professional basketball team: you sit on the bench and earn your keep without ever breaking a sweat, and you don't have to deal with the pressure of being in the limelight. But you don't experience the thrill, the satisfaction, the sheer pleasure of playing the game.

Fortunately, life is not like basketball in one crucial respect: you can put yourself in the game anytime you want. People who play the role of the twelfth player in life usually do so because they haven't taken time to choose a North Star. Setting goals, choosing objectives, and orienting your life around those goals and objectives is the only way to get yourself off the bench and into the game.

I frequently visit schools to speak to young people. I have a sincere desire to change the world, and I figure a good starting point is to help the next generation change its perspective on living. (This is one of the *giving* components of my vision.) Depending on the school, between four hundred and a thousand students pour into the gym or cafeteria. I stand on the stage—or occasionally on a table—and look out at youthful, enthusiastic faces. I know that most of those young people have no idea where they are or where they're going. And that is how many children end up in trouble: They just go with the flow, whatever the flow may be. *They never stop to check their compasses to identify what paths they're on and in what directions they're heading.*

I visited an elementary school in Sheffield, England, a town with high unemployment resulting from steel-plant closings years ago. I was scheduled to speak for an hour, but the kids were so interested in my message that the principal canceled classes for the rest of the day and I continued for five hours.

I began by asking the kids what they wanted to do when they finished school. Their answers were quite similar:

"I dunno."

"I dunno."

"I dunno."

"I dunno."

"I dunno."

"I dunno."

And then one girl said, "What my parents do, I suppose."

"And what is that?" I asked.

"They look for jobs," she said.

At first I thought she was joking—Brits have a more sarcastic sense of humor than Americans do—but she wasn't. So I brought her on stage, and in front of the audience she and I had a conversation about direction. I used her story, which many of the kids could relate to, as an example of failing to use your personal compass. During the five hours, I helped the kids grasp the compass concept, and they thought about where they were currently and in what direction they were heading. By the last hour, many kids had picked their North Stars and all had learned how to use their personal compasses. I was exhausted, but I had succeeded.

I've met successful attorneys who floated through college and law school simply because family and friends expected them to be lawyers. Then suddenly, at forty-five, they realize they don't know why they're sitting in nice offices in law firms in Minneapolis. They just wandered along the paths without examining their directions. They never consulted their compasses. They never rationally decided that the life of a successful attorney was the life they wanted or didn't want.

You can't know which path will take you to your final destination, because the world around you is in flux. But if you consult your compass frequently, you'll be able to take firm control of your life and put yourself back on track whenever you seem to be heading too far into the wilderness.

> *Your compass tells you which direction is north,*
> *and it's up to you to find the path to get there.*

*Just as energy is the basis
of life itself, and ideas the
source of innovation, so is
innovation the vital spark
of all man-made change,
improvement, and progress.*

Theodore Levitt (b. 1925)
Harvard Business School professor and author

Think for a moment about some of the most successful entrepreneurs of our day. For example, take Bill Gates, the founder and CEO of Microsoft. His software company single-handedly revolutionized the personal-computer industry. Gates is the undisputed leader of the computer-software industry because his innovative ideas have made personal computers an integral part of daily life for hundreds of millions of us.

Entrepreneurs are innovators. They conceive of, create, and develop new businesses and by extension spark the advent of changes in society. They are like adventurers who set sail on uncharted waters or who cut new paths through unexplored woods.

As an adventure entrepreneur, you, too, are an innovator. You have the ability and the opportunity to create new ideas. Use them to power your expedition toward the treasure. Don't be afraid to blaze a new trail in your community, your city, your industry, or in society as a whole.

Follow Your Instincts

Ralph Waldo Emerson said, "A man should learn to detect and watch that gleam of light which flashes across his mind from within. Yet he dismisses without notice his thought, because it is his. In every work of genius we recognize our own rejected thoughts: they come back to us with a certain alienated majesty." Emerson believed that every individual has the ability to generate new ideas and that everyone is capable of genius. We can make great strides if only we are self-reliant enough to trust our instincts.

Too often, potential adventure entrepreneurs never embark on their expeditions because they don't believe in the value of their ideas. They don't trust their instincts. They reject their ideas as trivial and unworthy of serious attention. They convince themselves that their ideas have no real value because otherwise someone else would have already tried it. *Entrepreneurs become successful not because they have genius-level IQs but because they have a tenacious belief in their ideas.*

Entrepreneurs thrive in the jungle of business by blazing new trails, by following their instincts. Self-confidence is the power characteristic of the entrepreneur. Even the best, most innovative idea will wither and blow away if it is not acted on with strength and conviction. You must have a strong belief in yourself and your ideas to transform your vision into reality.

Chris Whittle believed he was onto something. Six years ago, this Tennessee-based entrepreneur came up with an idea that proposed to transform the role of business in U.S. education. His concept was nothing short of revolutionary, and it was incredibly simple: using television to teach teenagers about national and world events, two areas largely untouched by classroom educators. He proposed to broadcast his news program, Channel One, into thousands of junior high and high school classrooms across the country every weekday morning. The twelve-minute broadcast would include two minutes of advertising—his profit from the enterprise.

Whittle's plan, of course, was met with considerable opposition from teachers, parents, and activists. His critics contended that bringing commercialism into the schools would undermine the validity of the education it espouses. Said one critic in *Newsweek*, "We should teach that life satisfaction is something more abstract than buying Dial soap." Whittle, on the other hand, maintained that the ads would not be harmful and that the introduction of television into the classrooms would only strengthen American education. Whittle's critics may or may not be right in assessing the ethics of his enterprise, and I won't pass judgment. But I will point out that Whittle is a model of self-confidence. He could easily have convinced himself that the idea would not work because large media corporations surely would have tried it if it were feasible. Or he could have shied away from the project by anticipating the hostile reaction of parents, teachers, and administrators.

Instead, he demonstrated tremendous belief in himself. He blazed his own trail in the education and media industries by conceptually combining the two in a simple yet effective way and then acting with strength and conviction. Although his ride has been bumpy, he has made the Channel One expedition successful; today the news program is broadcast into thousands of classrooms and generates several hundred million dollars in revenues every year.[1]

Charlie M. Leighton, founder and CEO of CML Group, has blazed a trail for twenty-five years. This innovative entrepreneur has built a wildly successful company by acquiring businesses that capitalize on consumer interests. For instance, Leighton bought the famous NordicTrack exercise machine from a Minneapolis couple in 1986. They had invented the exerciser to aid their daughter in her cross-country ski training. Leighton believed that a health movement was imminent and that people were far too busy to work out regularly in health clubs. So he followed his instincts and transformed the at-home exercise industry into a U.S. phenomenon.

Leighton brought NordicTrack into millions of homes by pioneering the use of direct advertising. He placed ads in magazines and newspapers, on television, and in catalogs, all of which feature a toll-free number so consumers can purchase NordicTrack immediately over the phone without going to a retail store.

Leighton turned his vision of an in-home exercise frenzy into a multimillion-dollar enterprise. But it would not have been possible if he had succumbed to doubt. He could have thought about how difficult it would be to sell a rather costly piece of exercise machinery to millions of Americans. But like all successful entrepreneurs, he maintained confidence in himself and blazed a new trail in product marketing. CML Group regularly advertises NordicTrack in practically every magazine on the news racks, on every television network, and in every major newspaper. Anyone with experience in the direct-marketing industry would have told Leighton he was crazy—that it's not possible to cover the costs of so many ads no matter *what* you're selling. But he believed in his concept and blazed a trail straight to a big treasure. Last year, his company sold $378 million of NordicTracks, about $98 million of which was operating profit.[2]

Neither were Hyman Golden and Leonard Marsh daunted by the prospect of a tough challenge. They built Snapple into a huge business because they never doubted the validity of their inner flashes of light. They seized a good idea and brought it to life.

Golden and Marsh started Snapple with an idea that was almost too simple. They believed that the major soft-drink companies, Pepsi and Coca-Cola, weren't capitalizing on a significant portion of the market. They believed that there must be many people who would prefer noncarbonated drinks to the popular sodas. So they built a company based on the production and mass-marketing of noncarbonated drinks—flavored iced teas and juices. There were already similar products on the market, but they were not mass-marketed like the major sodas are.

Golden and Marsh could have doubted their ingenuity, convinced themselves that the idea, if workable, surely would have been tested by the major corporations. After all, Coca-Cola and Pepsi have thousands of employees, many of whom work on marketing and product development. *But Golden and Marsh were the first to put the idea into action.* They had enough belief in themselves and their ideas to make it work. In fact, it worked so well that several years later sales skyrocketed to more than half a billion dollars.[3]

Never dismiss your ideas as trivial, unworthy, or invalid. Never reject your own vision. Have the courage to believe in yourself and your ideas. Blaze your own trail!

Stomp on the Fear of Rejection

Believing in your ideas is easy when they meet with immediate acceptance and widespread approval. However, maintaining confidence in yourself becomes much more difficult when your ideas are insulted and rejected.

Few innovative ideas, though, have been met with universal approval—just ask Chris Whittle! In fact, *expect to encounter disapproval, outright rejection, and condescending laughter from authoritative figures in your industry.* Perhaps even family and friends, the people who are closest to you, will also laugh at your vision.

In Switzerland I had a most enlightening dinner with a true trailblazer, a man who exemplifies the spirit of adventure entrepreneurship. Nicholas Hayek revolutionized the wristwatch industry and resuscitated a dying Swiss vocation by ignoring the scoffs of industry executives and an entire nation of doubters. In the mid-1980s, when Asian companies introduced a slew of smaller and cheaper watches, the Swiss turned to Hayek, then an engineering consultant, for help in formulating a strategy that would help them reclaim their place in the world watch market.

Hayek suggested that the Swiss do what the English had failed to do in the 1980s, when Japanese imports began to threaten their auto industry: take the focus of their business off high-end luxury models and redirect it toward inexpensive, mass-marketed, and mass-produced products. Threatened by inexpensive Japanese imported cars, the English put all their marbles on high-end luxury cars—Jaguar and Rolls-Royce. And the Japanese wiped them out.

Hayek explained that the best way to save the faltering industry was temporarily to stay away from the expensive luxury brands—Rolex and Omega, for example. The only way to secure the high-end market, Hayek told them, was to establish a firm hold on the low-end market. They needed to develop an inexpensive watch capable of being produced in large volume and sold to a wide segment of the world population.

But the watchmakers ridiculed him. They said the idea would never work. Hayek pitched the idea on Swiss national television and was received by a nation of doubters. If the idea was so great, the skeptics responded, Hayek should put his money where his mouth is. They wanted him to finance the bulk of the project. So he did!

Hayek created Swatch watches, which became an overnight sensation. Swatches became the best-selling inexpensive watch on the market within two years. And as Hayek predicted, his concept saved the Swiss watchmaking industry. Launched in 1983, Swatch sold 100 million watches by 1992 and has expanded production to include cellular phones, pagers, and other electronic devices. Hayek's idea was no flash in the pan; it continues to produce big dividends for the Swiss. Hayek has created thousands of jobs. Today, his company, SMH Swiss Corporation for Microelectronics and Watchmaking, profits not only from the Swatch brand but from the Omega, Rado, Longines, Tissot, Certina, Hamilton, and Mido lines as well—many of which he acquired from the people who insulted his original idea. And he is very proud of his accomplishments![4]

When the established leaders of the Swiss watch industry—the widely accepted authority—scorned him, and when the masses of people questioned him, Hayek continued to believe in himself. He never allowed lack of confidence to prohibit his vision from becoming reality.

Mark David Norris of Send Inc. encountered the same kind of skepticism from major greeting-card company executives when he approached them at the major card convention in New York City with his ideas for new, alternative designs. When he told me this inspiring story, I could hear the triumph in his voice.

Norris visited each of the hundreds of display booths on the convention floor. At various booths he asked the same question: "Instead of the standard rectangular cards with cute little flowers and sweet poems on the inside, couldn't you try printing square cards, cards with crazy, cool photos on the front, and cards with no message? You know, something different, unique?"

Repeatedly Norris heard chuckles and giggles, and occasionally the other companies' designers broke into laughter. "There's no market for cards like that," he heard over and over and over.

So what do you think he did? That's right. He went back to Philadelphia and began creating square cards with exciting photos and blank interiors. From his research, Norris had found that the major greeting-card companies were wrong. He had talked to customers, sales reps, and distributors, and he knew that the big companies were making a mistake.

Norris didn't listen to the laughter of the crowd. He had confidence in his own idea. Typically, small greeting-card companies print small sample runs of new cards. Norris believed in his idea and printed half a million cards in the first print run. His innovative concept propelled him into uncharted waters, and his confidence allowed him to blaze a new trail in the greeting-card industry.

Hayek and Norris powered their way to success by overcoming the doubt, ridicule, and scorn of skeptics. *Do not let the fear of rejection deter you from cutting a fresh path through the woods.* Show perseverance, determination, and conviction when you encounter a dense forest. Take out your machete and start carving your path!

The Trailblazing Lifestyle

Entrepreneurs are neither ultraconservative—dressed in red ties and gray suits—nor brash, flamboyant, and reckless—with slicked-back hair, round sunglasses, and L.A. tans. They are a diverse group of people who come in all ages and ethnicities and from all cultures and many walks of life. They work on different levels of business, some selling hot dogs on a downtown corner and others selling computer hardware on the world market.

Entrepreneurs aren't defined by what they sell, to whom they sell, or how much they earn. *Entrepreneurs are defined by who they are.* They live a particular lifestyle defined by the commitment to forego the traditional trail of employment to seek their treasure. They give up the staid security of a salaried position and the easy comfort of an hourly wage to brave the dangers of an adventure in the jungle of business. Entrepreneurship is, in itself, a trailblazing lifestyle.

By simply picking up this book and reading it, you have begun your adventure. There is an adventure entrepreneur inside you who wants to get out. You've traveled to the edge of the woods, and now you're ready to blaze your trail through the jungle of entrepreneurship.

Do not look for a path to follow.
Go instead where there is no path,
and leave fresh footprints in the soil.

PART IV

Preparing

for Your

Expedition

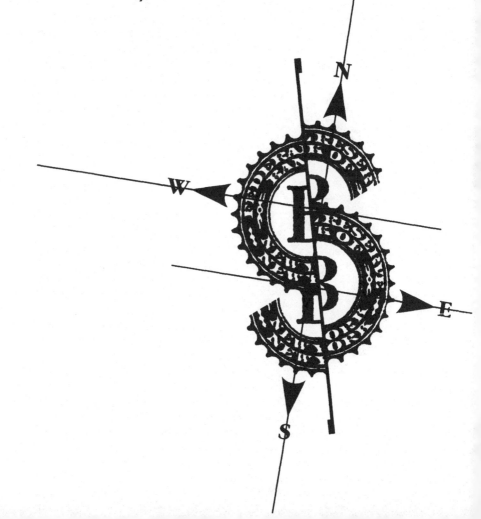

Introduction to Part IV

Preparation is the foundation of your venture adventure. In this stage, you determine where you want to go and how you're going to get there.

In my experience, 90 percent of the people starting businesses simply skip the preparation stage. They think of a business idea, run to city hall to get a business license, and open up. As a result, they may end up doing work they don't enjoy and making less than they had expected.

As a successful *adventure* entrepreneur, you will earn as much as you desire and enjoy every part of your company's growth. But first you must *envision your ideal lifestyle*, then *choose the business* and *assemble the team* that will help you create that lifestyle.

How long you spend preparing is not as important as how carefully you think about and delineate your strategy. If you decide to open a restaurant, your preparation stage may be six months to two years. In contrast, I've launched companies after one week of preparation.

When you have a clear picture of your destination and can envision which path will lead you there, you'll know you're ready to begin your adventure.

*We are more in need of a
vision or destination and a
compass (a set of principles
or directions) and less in
need of a road map.*

Stephen R. Covey (b. 1932)
American author

Perhaps she isn't one of the world's most renowned explorers, but she is, nonetheless, one of fiction's most charming travelers. When Alice finds herself lost in Wonderland, she looks to Lewis Carroll's many strange characters for help. Early in the novel, she sees the Cheshire Cat. The scene offers a good laugh and an interesting lesson:

> "Cheshire Puss," she began, rather timidly . . . "Would you tell me, please, which way I ought to go from here?"
>
> "That depends a good deal on where you want to get to," said the Cat.
>
> "I don't much care where—" said Alice.
>
> "Then it doesn't matter which way you go," said the Cat.[1]

To make effective decisions on your journey, you need to know your approximate destination. *If you don't know where you're going, you'll end up somewhere else!*

You need to create a *vision* of your destination, a mental image of your ideal life. In this chapter I'll help you construct your vision by helping you explore your personal and professional ambitions. With your vision in mind, you'll be able to design an exciting, fulfilling venture adventure that will enable you to achieve your dream lifestyle.

Defining Your Vision

Before you can realize your ideal lifestyle, you must develop a clear mental picture of it. Imagine you are going to build a house. Before you buy wood or pour concrete, you imagine exactly what your new house is going to look like. You'll probably convey that vision to an architect, who will put your mental image on paper in the form of architectural renderings. You can't start construction until you have a firm idea of the design and layout of the house. It would be ludicrous to buy a piece of land and bring in the cement trucks before you think about the house design. Similarly, starting on your venture adventure without a vision will result in wasted energy, time, and money. But if you begin with a defined vision, *you can take action to create an entrepreneurial expedition that will help you turn the mental image of your ideal lifestyle into reality*. The image you construct should be an *ideal* concept: your life and your business as they would be in a perfect world. Imagine what you *really want*, not what you *expect*.

As a fourteen-year-old grocery bagger at Super Foods supermarket in Montgomery, Alabama, Gregory Calhoun envisioned himself as its owner. Speaking about his vision, Calhoun told *Entrepreneur* magazine, "Nobody believed me. In 1968, black people in Montgomery couldn't even get managerial positions."

Calhoun kept this clear vision in the front of his mind, and nearly two decades later he purchased the Super Foods store he originally worked in, becoming the first African-American to own a major supermarket in the South. Today, his six-store empire employs more than five hundred people and grosses more than $50 million.[2] But his business, like a new house, was first an image and then a reality.

The following eight questions are brainteasers. They should prompt a vivid mental picture of your ideal lifestyle. As you proceed through the questions, let your imagination run wild. Ignore your current situation, both the negative and the positive aspects, so you can create an unbiased, true vision of your ideal lifestyle.

Where do you want to live? Be as specific as possible. Think about what part of the world you like the most. If possible, choose a particular city, even a certain neighborhood in that city. If you love excellent restaurants, perhaps you'll choose a major city like New York or San Francisco. If you prefer to catch your dinner, maybe you'll opt for living on a river in the Montana wilderness. (If you have conflicting interests, you can have two homes!)

In what kind of home do you want to live? Think in terms of style, size, and construction. If you have or plan to have children, you'll probably want a more spacious home with plenty of grass outside. Give consideration to the style—Victorian, Mediterranean, art deco, adobe, and so on. These questions are not designed to be materialistic. We spend a good portion of our lives in our homes, so I think they are an important component of our ideal lifestyles.

What kinds of friends do you want to have? You can surround yourself with anyone you wish. Do you want to hang out with movie stars or associate with world leaders in business and politics? (Remember, this is your *ideal* lifestyle.) Perhaps you would like to keep your childhood friends or stay close to your family. Think about whether you would like to have many acquaintances or just a few close friends. The people with whom you will associate will have an enormous impact on your ability to realize the other aspects of your ideal lifestyle.

What will be your daily routine? Maybe you'll wake up at seven, have a game of tennis, return and take a shower, and then have a light breakfast. Plan your ideal day, hour by hour. Think carefully about how much time you will allot to your business, your family, and yourself. Will you spend two hours per day working on your business, or closer to sixteen? Do you want to have your evenings free to spend at home with your family, or do you plan to hit the town every night? How much time do you want for yourself and for exercising, reading, and relaxing by the pool?

What will be your major sources of challenge and fulfillment? Money creates comfort, not fulfillment, so determine what kinds of activities will help you feel gratified, content, and satisfied with your existence. Starting and running your business may be the focus of your life. I know entrepreneurship itself can be very fulfilling. Perhaps, though, your source of challenge and fulfillment will be raising children, playing a sport, writing a book, or working on humanitarian projects.

What do you want to do with your money? Deciding what you want to do with your money will help you determine how much you need to make. Many people dream of Rockefeller-sized wealth, but in outlining how they would use the money, they decide they need just $150,000 a year, not the billion-and-a-half dollars they had imagined. The money you make from your business can be used in a variety of ways. Of course you can buy things for yourself and your family. You may want to put aside funds for your children or for future generations. You may want to have money so you can become a philanthropist and fund charitable programs. How much money you decide you want will help you choose the right business venture to launch.

How much and what kind of impact do you want to have on the people around you? What do you hope to gain from your relationships? . One of the most interesting places I have given a speech is the large, beautiful yard of a lakefront house near Dallas. An entrepreneur owns the home, and once a year he flies in the managers and team leaders of his company— about one hundred people—from around the country for a weekend retreat. He gets a tremendous amount of satisfaction from bringing them all together, instructing them, and motivating them. Perhaps you, too, would like to employ many people and have a positive impact on their lives.

How much and what kind of impact do you want to have on the world? Everyone makes an impact on the world, some in more visible ways than others. The spectrum ranges from Bill Gates, whose work in the computer industry is transforming the lives of people all around the globe, to a schoolteacher in a small town in Alabama, who is crafting the lives of fifteen children. How would you like your business and your efforts in the community to affect the world? Your business does not have to change the world to be worthwhile. Remember, if your efforts have an impact on just a few people, you will have a global effect as those people have an impact on a few more, who will have an impact on a few more . . .

I hope you have envisioned a lucid image of your ideal lifestyle. *The experience of launching and carrying out your business adventure should be organized around the eventual attainment of this lifestyle.* You'll want to launch a business that will allow you to afford the house you'd like to have, a business that can support your needs for challenge, fulfillment, and friendship or allow you enough time to pursue those needs elsewhere. You'll want a business that provides you with the money you want and allows you to have a positive effect on the people around you. *Business, unlike any other profession I know, can help you bring your ideal lifestyle to fruition quickly.*

For many people (including myself), running a business is in itself a fundamental part of the vision. Entrepreneurship allows me to live where I want, associate with leaders, design my daily routine, and have a positive effect on thousands of people. Entrepreneurship provides the challenges, the rewards, and the personal satisfaction many people search for all their lives. Entrepreneurship by itself can be the ideal lifestyle, or you can use entrepreneurship as a means to reach your ideal lifestyle.

Most important, though, by viewing your business experience as an adventure, you will enjoy the process of pursuing your goal. I have helped you create a vision not so you will march relentlessly to reach your destination but rather so you will know in which direction to head when you begin your journey and when you encounter obstacles along the way.

Determining Your Business Adventure

Now let's use your ideal lifestyle image to determine the kind of business adventure that's right for you.

After you've created a vision, make it your North Star. Use your vision as a fixed point to find your relative location and to chart your progress. Frequently stop and take note of where you are—orient yourself with respect to your North Star. If the direction you're traveling in is no longer bringing you closer to your North Star, change directions. Monitor your expedition to make sure you are on course for achieving your dreams.

The purpose of a vision is to ensure that your efforts are well spent, that you are working with a mission in mind. In *The Seven Habits of Highly Effective People*, Stephen Covey writes, "It's incredibly easy to get caught up in an activity trap, in the busy-ness of life, to work harder and harder at climbing the ladder of success only to discover it's leaning against the wrong wall. It is possible to be busy—very busy—without being effective."[3]

The key word in this passage is *effective*. Without a crisp, clear vision of your ideal lifestyle, your efforts in business and in life will not be effective. Creating an image of your ideal lifestyle before you embark is important not only because it will help you make decisions during your journey but also because you just might reach your destination!

A vision is not the same thing as a business plan. A business plan describes steps to achieving a goal. It contains timetables, figures, and other specifics. The basic premise of a business plan is that it will forecast every stage of your business experience. But it is not possible to foresee all the stages of a venture adventure. That's what makes the experience exciting!

Conventional business plans lead you down a straight-and-narrow path, leaving too little freedom to accommodate unexpected changes. Following a business plan is similar to adopting the mentality of a frightened ostrich. When threatened by attack, the ostrich tries to escape by running toward the windward end of the valley. And the bird adheres rigidly to this plan. Livingstone wrote that the natives "commence running, as if to cut off his [the ostrich's] retreat from the passage through which the wind blows; and although free to go out at the opposite outlet, he madly rushes forward to get past the men, and is speared."[4]

The ostrich clearly has a vision: to escape. And it has a plan to realize that vision: to run to the windward end of the valley. The problem is that the ostrich commits itself to a rigid plan and refuses to be flexible to accommodate changes. It blindly adheres to its plan, even though a simple adjustment—running the other way—would allow it to escape easily.

Fortunately, you have instincts, reflexes, and mental abilities far more advanced than those of the ostrich, so put them to good use! Do not formulate a detailed business plan that will lock you into a mad dash toward your destination. Create your vision, point yourself in the right direction, and enjoy the adventure of pursuing your vision.

After being laid off from his job as a shoe salesman in a department store, Kelly Thayer had an idea for a video production and duplication business. He had no prior experience in the business, and he didn't have the money to hire a professional firm to help him get started. So Thayer turned to an MBA class at Brigham Young University to create a business plan for him.

The class analyzed his idea, produced a business plan, and concluded that his company would fail. Undaunted, Thayer launched his business with just $600. Today, Orem, Utah-based Clear Image boasts more than $800,000 in annual pretax profits.[5] *Not bad for a company with a business plan that predicted it would fail!*

General Robert E. Wood, president of Sears, Roebuck & Company for many years, said, "Business is like war in one respect. If its grand strategy is correct, any number of tactical errors can be made and yet the enterprise proves successful." In other words, if your vision is strong, you don't have to worry about the details of reaching it. Trust in your ability, instincts, and quick reflexes to get you there.

Remember to maintain a flexible vision. In the autumn of 1492, as Columbus sailed westward from Europe, he entertained visions of reaching the treasures of the East Indies. He carried with him the hopes of the king and queen of Spain, who funded his exploration and hoped to profit from his journey. In fact, many Europeans hoped that Columbus would open a fast, easy passage to those treasures.

In the early morning hours of October 12, 1492, Rodrigo de Triana, lookout on the *Pinta*, yelled "*Tierra! Tierra!*" ("Land! Land!"). He had glimpsed small flashes of the Bahamas. Columbus had realized the hopes of the Europeans—sort of. He hadn't found a westward passage to the East Indies but rather a continent new to the Europeans' understanding of the world.[6] The Europeans changed their outlook to accommodate the discovery. Their goal was to find a western passage to Asia, but along the way they found something much more interesting. They were flexible with their vision and willing to adapt it to changing circumstances.

You, too, may reach your treasure before you attain your original vision. Perhaps your business will generate profits much more quickly than you expected. Perhaps you will find a new venture—manufacturing glow-in-the-dark shoelaces, for example—that proves to be fulfilling and lucrative. Unexpected changes in the landscape of the jungle may cause you to rethink your vision, to modify your concept of your ideal lifestyle.

You may decide that you want to devote a significantly larger chunk of your time and energy to philanthropic activities. You may determine that you need to make more money so that you can buy your mother a Corvette. Conversely, you may discover that you don't need to earn huge bucks to be happy; you may decide to scale back to a smaller enterprise, as Bob and Cindy Maynard did (see Chapter 18).

Your vision is not a permanent, concrete fixture. It is a flexible concept that can and should be rethought, adjusted, and corrected as you travel on your adventure. Your vision is a general idea of how your business can help you achieve your ideal lifestyle, not a detailed list of accomplishments you hope to have realized by a certain time.

Visioning is your opportunity to craft a mission, a purpose, for your journey. First, create a mental picture of your perfect lifestyle that incorporates your professional, personal, and emotional ambitions. Then, be flexible with your vision. Revise it as you proceed on your adventure. Use it as a North Star for your expedition. Use your vision to determine the course of your business and to help you make decisions along the way.

***Like a dream home, your ideal life begins as a vision,
and later, through skillful construction, it becomes a reality.***

> *Pleasure in the job puts*
> *perfection in the work.*   Aristotle

Allow me to get straight to the point. The best way to choose a business is to find something that you feel passionate about and turn it into an enterprise. If you can quickly identify your favorite activity—playing tennis, exploring new computer technology, reading fiction, whatever—you'll be able to create an exciting, rewarding business venture.

I think this is everyone's dream—to be able to do what you love all day, every day. The large majority of people work eight hours a day, five days a week in relatively unsatisfying jobs so they can earn money to spend a little time doing what they love. Example: Joaquim works full time for a major corporation preparing cost-analysis reports—a rather tedious chore—because the job pays well. Khalese, his wife, is manager of a bank branch and also draws a very good salary. Their earnings allow them to live comfortably and, much more important to them, to spend every Saturday and Sunday boating.

By regular standards, this couple is doing well—they have jobs, a small home, two cars, and a boat. Joaquim and Khalese each work forty hours a week, and they do their favorite activity, boating, about sixteen hours a week. But I don't think this is an ideal lifestyle. *Life is too short to have a 5:2 work-to-play ratio.*

Now imagine if Joaquim and Khalese opened a boating-supplies store on a nearby lake. Sure, it would be a risky move to give up two good jobs to start a business. But with their passion for boating, J & K Boating Stuff Inc. would probably succeed. Not only would their joint income eventually *increase*, but they would be able to spend seven days a week at the lake, not just two. Like any venture adventure, their business would be challenging, but they would be doing what they love. Joaquim and Khalese would be living a dream.

Imagine waking up knowing you'll spend the entire day doing your favorite activity, whatever it is. The great free-enterprise system makes that kind of life possible. You have the power to create a dream lifestyle for yourself, and choosing the right business is the first step.

Turn Enjoyment to Enterprise

When you successfully turn a favorite activity into an enterprise, running your company won't seem like work, no matter how many hours you spend on business. Management guru Tom Peters, in his book *The Pursuit of Wow!* writes, "Business ceases to be work when you're chasing a dream that has engorged you."[1] Running a business you feel passionate about will instill so much energy and happiness in your life that you'll look forward to getting up every morning.

When Mark McCormack launched his company, International Management Group, he certainly didn't envision leading a firm with fifteen offices around the world and revenues in excess of $200 million. In fact, his goal was rather simple. In his book of business advice, *What They Don't Teach You at Harvard Business School,* McCormack recalled, "I was a young lawyer simply looking for a way to combine one of my lifelong passions—golf—with my day-to-day business activities." So he came up with the idea of being a representative for players on the PGA tour. Voilà! His sports-management firm was born. Today, the company represents athletes in many sports, organizes sporting events, consults with large corporations, and owns two leading fashion-model agencies.[2] McCormack is good at what he does because he loves the world of sports.

Not only does running a business that you feel passionate about help you feel good, it increases your chances of earning big bucks. In his book *If It Ain't Broke . . . Break It!* mental coach Robert Kriegl cited a fascinating investigative study. Researchers followed the lives of 1,500 people for about twenty years. At the beginning of the study, 83 percent—about 1,245 people—opted for money-making careers right away, deciding to wait until later to pursue happiness. The remaining 17 percent—about 255 people—decided to do something that made them happy first and worry about money later.

When the twenty-year period had elapsed, the researchers found some surprising results. Of the original 1,500 people, 101 had become millionaires. But only one of those millionaires came from the group of 1,245 people who chose to make money right away. One hundred people from the second group, roughly 40 percent of the 255 people who chose to pursue happiness first, ended up millionaires. "Research reveals," Kriegl wrote, "that the more you love what you do, the better you'll do it and the more money you'll make."[3]

Billy Thompson followed his heart's desire and turned his boyhood hobby into a thriving business. His company, White Post Restorations, today is one of the top antique-car renovation firms in the nation.

"I've loved old cars since I was twelve, when I bought my first one," Thompson explained to me. While driving with his parents, he spotted a 1940 Ford convertible in a used-car lot in Woodstock, Virginia, thirty miles south of his home. He talked his friend's older brother into driving him back to the lot.

So twelve-year-old Billy encountered his first used-car salesman, who quickly announced that he would take nothing less than $50 for the old car that didn't run. Billy said that he had only $35 to spend. The salesman walked into his office and returned with the title and the receipt. Billy and his friend's brother *towed* the car home!

Thompson admits that his parents went through the roof. But his love affair with antique cars had begun, and everything else fell easily into place.

When he was eighteen, Thompson inherited his father's four-bay auto garage in White Post, Virginia. His passion for cars showed in the quality of his work, and his business quickly outgrew the four bays. Today the researchers, body workers, mechanics, and machinists of White Post Restorations work in a huge building—about half an acre under one roof, Thompson likes to point out. As a reward for spending his days doing what he loves, Thompson is earning some good money. His business will gross nearly $2 million this year.

Thompson has crafted an ideal lifestyle for himself. He said, "To pursue success, most people get in a car and drive thirty-seven miles to work. I wake up and commute thirty-seven steps to my office." From his desk, he has a stunning view of the Blue Ridge Mountains. His company employs twenty people and therefore touches twenty families. White Post Restorations is the pride of White Post, Virginia (population fifty—I'm not kidding); car enthusiasts from as far away as Greece, Japan, and Venezuela bring their automobiles to Thompson's firm to be restored.

Thompson vocalized what all true adventure entrepreneurs feel: "I get to work an hour earlier than I should, because I love what I do."[4] You'll know you found the right business when your alarm is set for 7:00 A.M. and you open your eyes at six o'clock.

The Lesson of the Perennial Stream

Livingstone was an astute observer of the landscape through which he traveled. At one point in his explorations, he encountered a stream about forty yards wide and moving fairly fast. He observed quickly that it was "a perennial stream as the existence of hippopotami proves."[5] Many streams in the area ran dry during the summer. But he determined that this stream flowed all year because hippos would not be living in it if it ever ran dry. The lesson of the perennial stream teaches us a valuable strategy for choosing a business.

Here is the biggest mistake people make when choosing a business to start: They come up with a business idea, do some research, and find that several companies are already doing either something very similar or exactly what they had planned on. So they drop that idea and search for another. *But the presence of established companies offering your product or service is a great sign, not a reason to discard it.*

When several hippos are living comfortably around a stream, it means that the stream is capable of supporting life! If there are some old hippos lingering around the stream, that's even better—it indicates the stream has been flowing for a long time.

In business, the presence of competitors in an industry you're examining is *good news*. It is a sign that other companies are making money selling the product or service you're thinking of selling. The hippos Livingstone spotted chose a wide, deep, swift stream to call home. You'll want to do the same thing. *Launch your business in a growing, thriving industry.* If there are plenty of well-established competitors already in the stream, don't let that deter you. Rather, consider it an indication that the stream can support more life.

It Doesn't Have to Be New

David and Greg Figueroa certainly didn't invent hot sauce. Tabasco had been around for many years before they arrived, but the Figueroa brothers created a new niche in an old industry. They made a splash in the hot-sauce market by introducing Melinda's Original Habanero Pepper Sauce, the first made with habanero peppers instead of with traditional chili peppers.

When the Figueroas launched their venture adventure, Tabasco controlled 98 percent of the hot-sauce market, and a plethora of small companies competed for the remaining 2 percent. But all their products looked similar. David told me, "The first thing we did was go down to the supermarket and look at the other hot sauces on the shelf. And they were all pretty much the same: 'Hotter Than Hell Hot Sauce,' 'Red Devil Hot Sauce,' and 'Scorching Red Hot Sauce.'"

The brothers set out to make a distinctive gourmet hot sauce, "the Dom Perignon of hot sauces," as David put it. They wanted their product to look like the most expensive sauce on the shelf. In designing the package, they used red and green, strong food colors, and a trace of gold for the gourmet touch. Their strategy has paid off.

Melinda's, according to David, is now the number-two hot sauce on the market, with a 5 percent share (5 percent may not sound like a lot, but 5 percent of a huge market is still huge!). Meanwhile, Tabasco has slid from 98 percent to 85 percent. Today, Figueroa International Inc. sells the original Melinda's sauce, several other versions of the famous product, an herbed olive oil, dips, and salsas. The combined sales of their operations are about $200,000 per month.[6]

Domino's didn't invent pizza. But it made a name for itself by being the first to offer a thirty-minute delivery guarantee. Debbie Fields didn't invent cookies. But she was the first to create a national chain of cookie stores. Your business idea doesn't have to be brand-new to be good. Many of the most famous entrepreneurs simply put new twists on old ideas.

Love Your Product

Your expedition will survive in the jungle only if you feel enthusiastic about your product. Enthusiasm is contagious. Your excitement will arouse the confidence, anticipation, and positive energy in customers that impel them to purchase a product. (I use the word *product* loosely. Your product may be a service, too.)

When you examine possible businesses, keep in mind that your belief in your product is paramount to your company's success. No matter how much opportunity there is in the decorative-toilet-handle industry, if you can't get excited about toilet handles, your venture will not remain in business for the long term. On the other hand, if decorative toilet handles are your life's passion, you'll probably make a lot of money and a have a great time doing it.

To lead a successful venture adventure, you must know your product inside out. Business, at its core, is selling a product. And there are three areas you must know about your product if you are going to sell it successfully.

Tangible features. Know how your product works. Be familiar with all its functions and capabilities. If you're going to sell cellular phones, for instance, you need to know what functions they can perform, what functions they can't perform, and which buttons control which functions.

A cellular-phone store had a large poster in the window advertising a new model with, as the ad said, "cutting-edge functions." I strolled in and asked the man behind the counter, who turned out to be the owner, if he could show me the new phone. He proudly led me to a small display and put the phone in my hand.

"It's very light," he said.

"It is," I agreed. "And what are the hot new functions?"

"Oh, it's totally redesigned."

"Yes, I see that," I said, sensing he didn't know exactly what the new functions were. I pointed to a red button. "What does this button do?"

"Hold on," he said, "I'll check." And he went behind the counter and pulled out the manual. After about three minutes, he was still flipping through pages. I decided that if the phone was so complicated he couldn't figure it out, I certainly didn't have the time to work on it. So I thanked him and left.

Intangible features. You need to understand the concept—the idea— behind your product. Ask yourself, "What need does this product fulfill?" If you plan to sell the product effectively, you must know *what needs it will satisfy* and *what desires it will satiate*. If you don't know why customers should purchase your product, they won't, either.

Public perceptions. Equally important as knowing the tangible and intangible features of your product is thoroughly understanding how the public perceives it. You must be objective in identifying the preconceived opinions, both negative and positive, that customers may hold about it. You want to know the negative feelings so you can dispel them. And you want to know the positive feelings so you can publicize them.

Traditional business judgment suggests you sell whatever people will buy. *Adventure entrepreneurship urges selling something you feel good about, something that has meaning for you.* Remember, adventure entrepreneurship is making money *and* having the time of your life doing it. Selling decorative toilet handles may fulfill the making-money part, but if toilet handles don't have meaning for you, you won't be experiencing the true venture adventure.

The Feasibility Test

The first thing I do when I get an idea for a business is determine if it is capable of earning profits—otherwise, all other considerations are moot.

You need a few minutes and some simple tools: your common sense, a calculator, a piece of paper, and a pencil. Therefore, you can do this analysis anywhere, whenever you come up with a business idea. I recently thought of a great business for a new entrepreneur to launch. I was in a taxi in Cairo, and I ran the *feasibility test* in the back seat of a cab while racing through the craziest streets in the world.

How many times have you experienced deficient or downright awful service? Probably too many to count. How many times have you promised yourself you'd write a complaint letter? Again, probably too many to count. But how many times have you actually sat down and written a complaint letter, found the address to send it to, stamped it, and mailed it? Probably very few times. Enter my business idea, Complaints Inc.

Customers call an 800 number (preferably 1-800-COMPLAIN or something just as catchy) whenever they are upset with a product or a service. An operator or a good voice-mail system records their complaint (and their credit-card number). For a fee of $10, Complaints Inc. finds the right address and person to whom to send the complaint, writes a formal complaint letter, and mails it.

The company would have to advertise very little, because newspapers, magazines, and radio and television shows would provide plenty of free publicity. (This is the kind of business the media loves to feature.) Further, Complaints Inc. might publish an annual book of the funniest complaints, generating extra revenue and more publicity.

So the idea seemed quite good, but as with all my business ideas, I quickly ran the feasibility test. Here was my thinking process. I imagined Complaints Inc. could start as a one-person business aiming for $50,000 in annual profits. Expenses would amount to about $1.50 per letter (the cost of the envelope, letterhead, postage stamp, 800-number usage, and credit-card processing fees), so profit per complaint would be approximately $8.50. To realize $50,000 in profits the first year, Complaints Inc. would have to process 5,882 complaints ($5,882 \times \$8.50 = \$49,997$). That is about sixteen complaints every day of the year.

Feasible? Yes. *The numbers show that the venture is capable of making money.* The feasibility test quickly shows whether a business is likely to earn $100, $1,000, $100,000, or $1 million. To earn $1 million in operating profits, Complaints Inc. would have to process 322 complaints every day of the year. Feasible? You decide.

See how quickly I can decide on the feasibility of a business idea? Yet many people invest big bucks to start businesses without taking a couple of minutes to run this analysis.

The Five Characteristics of an Ideal Business

This isn't one of those fluffy quizzes where 1 means "bad," 2 means "less than average," 3 means "OK," 4 means "pretty good," and 5 means "the best." This one is all-or-nothing. If your business idea is missing any of the following characteristics, it isn't an ideal business for you. Period. On the other hand, if you think you and your business clearly possess all five characteristics, you can be confident you've found the right venture adventure for *you*.

Passion. Do you feel passionate about your business and your product? Your business should have special meaning for you. You should have a tremendous amount of enthusiasm for your venture, an intense desire to make the business successful. *Passion* keeps you going when the venture adventure becomes challenging. And passion is infectious. Your employees, suppliers, and customers will pick up your enthusiasm for your product.

Purpose. Does your business have a *purpose* of which you can be proud? This could apply either to the direct benefits of your product or to the indirect benefits you bring to society. Purpose is a predecessor of fulfillment. When your business has a distinct purpose (or several purposes), your venture adventure becomes fulfilling.

Particularity. Does your product or service have a special twist that makes it unique in the marketplace? Your business has to be *particular*, slightly different from the other companies in your industry, to thrive. *Your business must have an edge.* In the Plaka, a vibrant section of Athens filled with shops and stalls, the restaurants look the same, have similar names, and serve the same food for almost the same prices. At the first restaurant we saw, we stopped to look at the menu, and an enthusiastic restaurateur ran out and announced, "We have Greek salads, fish, *moussaka, pastitsio*, . . . everything you could want!" We continued to stroll and found another restaurant about fifteen feet down the street. As we looked at the menu, the restaurateur ran out, excited, and announced, "We have Greek salads, fish, *moussaka, pastitsio*, . . . everything you could want!" This happened over and over. Finally, I caught on. We approached another restaurant, started looking through the menu, and the owner ran out. But before he could say anything, I announced, "You have Greek salads, fish, *moussaka, pastitsio*, . . . everything we could possibly want!" And he simply said, "Exactly!" The problem was not that the restaurateurs in Athens know only one sentence in English. (Most speak perfect English.) The problem was that the restaurants in the Plaka lack the *particularity* characteristic. They are all practically the same, so the owners describe their businesses in practically the same way. As a result, all the restaurateurs seem to make a living, but not one makes a fortune. *Your product or service doesn't have to be different, but it must be distinctive. You have to give customers a reason to patronize your company instead of your competitors.*

Perpetuation. Is your company positioned to remain in business indefinitely? Of course, in the jungle you might encounter unexpected challenges that threaten your company, but this is natural for any business. *Possessing the perpetuation characteristic at the launch of a business means foreseeing the absence of any major events that may wipe it out.* For instance, the entrepreneur who opens an umbrella store during a rare rainy spring knows from the beginning of her enterprise that the market will soon dry up—the rain will stop and people will no longer need umbrellas. Her business concept does not possess the perpetuation characteristic. However, if she were to expand her product line to include bathing suits and scarves as well as umbrellas, her company would be able to serve customers during all seasons and therefore would be positioned to remain in business indefinitely.

Potential. Does your business have growth potential? Is your company a retail concept (a restaurant, dry cleaner, or clothing store, for example) that you can perfect and then duplicate in every U.S. city? Is your company a mail-order business that can begin by selling in your state and then expand across the nation and around the world? I'll be honest. I've never seen a company that doesn't have growth potential. Unless you've created a bizarre business concept, your company probably possesses the *potential* characteristic. But the challenge is identifying the avenues for possible expansion *at the beginning of your venture adventure.* Then you can keep those growth strategies in mind as you develop your business and begin to implement them as your company becomes successful.

If you and your business possess the five characteristics—passion, purpose, particularity, perpetuation, and potential—you can be confident that your venture adventure will be exciting, fulfilling, and rewarding. When you run a business you love, your enthusiasm shows.

If your business is your pleasure,
you will never have to mix business and pleasure.

*Never doubt that a small
group of thoughtful,
committed people can change
the world. Indeed, it is the
only thing that ever has.*

Margaret Mead (1901–1978)
American anthropologist

After visioning your future and choosing a business, you need to determine who is going to accompany you on your venture adventure. Most entrepreneurs start by themselves and assemble their teams as their companies grow. Many others, though, choose to find partners to complement their strengths and compensate for their weaknesses. Entrepreneurs in certain industries, like restaurants, hire a crew from the start. (It's tough for one person to greet customers, cook, serve, clear tables, wash dishes, and attend the cash register all at once!) The process of finding the right colleagues and the best personnel is difficult, but it is imperative to the success of your expedition.

The Solo Expedition

Thoreau said, "The man who goes alone can start today; but he who travels with another must wait till that other is ready, and it may be a long time before they get off." Entrepreneurship is, in itself, a fairly individualistic pursuit, and the one-person business boasts many luxuries. Free from the demands of partners and employees, the solo entrepreneur can lead a small expedition in any direction, at any time of day, and at any chosen speed.

But let us not contrive a false, romantic image of solo entrepreneurs—heroic adventurers who opt to explore the jungle by themselves because they are curious, eager, and daring. In starting new businesses, some entrepreneurs don't need any help, but *most simply cannot afford it.* (Employees are very expensive!) So the large majority of entrepreneurs launch their businesses by themselves and, as their bank accounts permit, then hire workers.

As you begin your venture adventure, you may feel that your company's lack of employees is a hindrance to fast growth. To the contrary, your inability to afford a payroll is actually a blessing in disguise. In the early stages of your venture adventure, going solo has many advantages. You can focus your vision, develop your company, and establish firm relationships without worrying about meeting a payroll. Beginning as a one-person business allows you to become comfortable with the power you wield as an individual, independent entrepreneur.

Solo adventurers can concentrate on maintaining their quickness, agility, and perception—all features imperative to jungle survival. Japanese adventurer Naomi Uemura used the do-it-yourself strategy in launching a solo expedition to the North Pole. With his supplies, a handcrafted oak sled, and a team of seventeen sled dogs, he trekked across the frozen arctic wasteland braving icy waters, incredibly cold air temperatures, and polar bears.

Huge ice boulders frequently challenged him. Using an iron bar, he hacked tight passages through the boulders just large enough for his dogs and him to scramble through. An expedition team of ten people would have spent many hours carving passages large enough to accommodate heavy sleds containing the team's food and clothing.

Then, too, Uemura had to contend with leads, the open lanes of water between ice floes. He would lug his one-thousand-pound sled and his seventeen dogs onto an ice block and slowly, carefully, row the makeshift raft across the deadly lead. Those maneuvers were particularly harrowing; one dip in the water spelled certain death. A ten-person crew would have rowed an ice block back and forth across the leads because too much weight on an ice raft might topple it. Not only would multiple maneuvers take more time, but they would force the crew members to repeatedly risk their lives instead of crossing the water only once.

Uemura's closest brush with death came one sullen, windswept night as he slept in his small nylon tent. Suddenly, he was awakened by the frenzied howls of his dogs outside. "There are few creatures a sled dog instinctively fears," Uemura wrote. "One is man, another is the polar bear." He knew his dogs' howls meant only one thing: a polar bear!

Uemura could hear the snarls of the beast as it tore through his supplies. He regretted not having loaded his rifle before he went to sleep—it lay useless at his side. Death seemed imminent when the animal ripped a hole in the tent, seemingly bent on further nourishment. Uemura curled up inside his sleeping bag as if dead. Miraculously, the beast only nudged him before it departed. Had there been several men in the tent, the bear would not have been fooled so easily. At least one of them would have likely been attacked. But as a solo adventurer, Uemura was able to survive the incident unharmed.

In fifty-five days Uemura covered 476 miles and became the first person to make a successful solo expedition to the North Pole.[1] He survived the harrowing adventure and reached his destination thanks largely to the advantages he gained by traveling alone—*the same advantages you, as a solo adventure entrepreneur, will enjoy in building a new business by yourself.*

- *You make quick decisions.* When you don't have to consult with partners or employees, you can react to challenges *immediately.* You can rely on *your* ingenuity, experience, and intuition to guide you through the jungle of entrepreneurship.
- *You move at your own pace.* When you feel a surge of motivation to work until two in the morning, you can. When you feel like taking a day off to go to the beach, you can—you don't have to notify anyone. As a solo adventurer, you don't have to speed up or slow down to accommodate your crew.
- *You travel lighter.* When journeying with a full crew, adventurers like Livingstone and Peary had to bring heavy loads full of supplies—ammunition, medicines, food, clothing, cooking equipment. Supplies are quite expensive, and carrying such a large quantity slows the whole expedition. In the early stages of a business, a large payroll is like a heavy sled. You have to worry about having enough cash to pay your employees, so you cannot devote your full attention to growing the business.
- *You enjoy the feeling of accomplishment.* When you launch and develop a business by yourself, you alone are responsible for its fate. When it thrives, you know you succeeded as a result of *your* effort. And the feeling of individual accomplishment is invigorating and motivating. Successfully developing a company with a partner is like winning a football game, but successfully establishing a company by yourself is like winning a singles tennis match.

As your company grows, inevitably you will need to hire employees. They will take care of the day-to-day operation, allowing you to concentrate on the growth and direction of your business. But in the meantime, you can enjoy the freedom and agility of solo adventuring in the jungle of entrepreneurship.

Partners

Partnerships offer some distinct advantages over sole proprietorships and single-owner corporations. You have more intellectual firepower—the experiences, knowledge, and imaginations of two or more people rather than one. You share the monetary risk. You brainstorm together to find more creative approaches to advertising, marketing, and customer service.

But partnerships certainly have some disadvantages. Practically every decision requires a conversation with your partner. You will spend a lot of time (read: a good part of your life) with your partner. You will have conflicts—most frequently over what to spend money on. When you make money, you'll have to share it. (This is the part that bothers most people!) But each partnership is different. In some cases the advantages outweigh the disadvantages, and in other cases the negatives prevail over the positives. You have to decide whether in your situation working with a partner will help or hinder you.

Your relationship, both personal and professional, with your partner will have a momentous effect on the progress of your entrepreneurial journey. I have studied and consulted with participants in some very successful and quite a few not-so-successful partnerships and have identified four distinct attributes of a healthy entrepreneurial alliance. Make sure you and your partner, whether a spouse, longtime friend, or industry expert, fulfill these criteria for a productive, long-lasting partnership.

Complementary skills. Good partnerships are a union of differing strengths. Depending on your experience and training, you will be stronger in some areas of your business and weaker in others. Likewise, your partner will have strengths and weaknesses. *In the ideal partnership, your strengths will compensate for your partner's weaknesses, and vice versa.*

Two young Boston-based entrepreneurs, Steven Shulman and Michael Yanoff, created a booming business, Cover Concepts Marketing Services Inc., by combining their strengths. Shulman had spotted a book cover that contained ads from local small businesses on one of his cousin's high school textbooks and was intrigued by this innovative marketing idea. He pondered the concept and began envisioning the idea on a national level. Instead of soliciting ads from the local pizzeria, why not go after Nike, Coca-Cola, and other big corporations interested in targeting school-age consumers? And instead of distributing the covers in local high schools, why not take the covers into every elementary, junior high, and high school in the nation?

At the time, Shulman was working at a shoe-importing company designing and packaging shoeboxes. He was confident in his ability to supervise the *design* aspect of the book-cover business, *but he didn't have experience selling advertising space.*

Shulman knew he needed help, so he thought about forming a partnership with Yanoff. They had been friends since they were children, and Yanoff had the ideal expertise to complement Shulman's skills. Yanoff was working for a local sports-radio station selling ad time to area businesses. *He knew how to sell advertising.*

The duo launched their venture adventure by selling ad space to companies like Nike, Maxell, and Coca-Cola, printing the book covers, and distributing them to high schools in their native Massachusetts. They received such positive feedback from the original high schools and advertisers that they went national just two years later.

Last year, Cover Concepts Marketing Services Inc. printed 40 million book covers with advertisements from nearly 100 companies. The covers reached 22 million students in 32,000 schools across the nation. Sales topped $4 million, with after-tax profits of up to 20 percent. That's somewhere in the range of $750,000 in profits—not bad for a five-year-old company. And Shulman and Yanoff still get along; even after long days at the office, they occasionally go out for a drink together.[2]

Compatible personalities. Douchan Gersi, a modern-day adventurer, deliberated quite heavily before choosing a partner to accompany him on his journey to the rugged areas of Borneo. "It is hard to choose the perfect companion for an expedition," he writes in his book *Explorer*. "Companions must, in personality and in skills, complement each other and yet be of the same spiritual caliber and level."[3]

From his experiences in the jungle, Gersi had learned that partners must be compatible in personality as well as in ability, courage, and drive. Adventurers traveling together in the wilderness often face life-threatening situations. They must think similarly, because the actions of one affect the safety of both. As well, adventurers working together in the jungle of business encounter frequent challenges and impediments. They, too, must have similar thinking patterns; each partner acts on behalf of a company in which both have significant emotional and financial investments.

You will share the ups and the downs with your partner. Your entrepreneurial expedition certainly will encounter rough terrain, obstacles, and pitfalls. And you'll experience the thrill of accomplishment. During the exciting and the discouraging stages of your adventure, you'll appreciate working with a partner who has a compatible personality.

Diversified tasks. Greg Figueroa originally came up with the idea for marketing hot sauce. He formed a partnership with his brother, David, and together they launched Figueroa International Inc. From the beginning, each brother had a separate role in the company, and they still maintain this effective division of labor. David handles all the creative work; he oversees the package and label design for the company's products. Greg is in charge of the administrative work—sales, finance, and personnel.

David recognizes the strength of their partnership. He told me, "We couldn't do it without each other. We're lucky to be a team with diverse talents."[4]

Shared vision. Irv Robbins and Burt Baskin went to great lengths to make certain they shared the same vision before they decided to become business partners. Following the advice of Irv's father, who told them that working together from the start would force them to compromise their individual ideas in an effort to get along, the two men opted to begin separate businesses. Each would have the freedom to experiment with his own ideas and strategies and to create a definitive vision of his ideal business.

After working solo for about a year, they decided to become partners—to launch a venture adventure together. They named their business Baskin-Robbins. And according to Joseph and Suzy Fucini, authors of the book *Entrepreneurs*, their "union was a harmonious one from the start, since both shared the same basic marketing philosophy—to sell nothing but ice cream and to offer a multitude of flavors." Even better, they shared the spirit of adventure entrepreneurship. Robbins said, "We just wanted to make $75 a week. And we wanted to enjoy ourselves doing it."

Baskin and Robbins worked in concert with the same vision and the same spirit to build Baskin-Robbins Ice Cream into an international corporation that dishes out twenty million gallons of ice cream in more than two thousand stores every year![5] From the start, they had the same vision—to sell good ice cream and to have fun doing it. *And they turned their vision into reality.*

Hiring Crew

Although you may choose to begin your venture adventure alone, at some point—the sooner the better—you'll have to hire employees. A significant new client, a steady increase in sales, a growing customer base, or the addition of a new location will require you to seek help fast. This is a rather momentous point in your venture adventure, a true mark of accomplishment. But the process of hiring isn't as easy as placing an ad in the help-wanted section of your local paper. Many business thinkers believe that the process of building and maintaining a team is the business owner's *most vital task.*

When you interview potential employees, watch for two qualifying factors. The first is the most beautiful of human assets—the smile. A smile is a nonverbal gesture of friendliness, an outward extension of a positive personality. If your employees will be interacting with customers face-to-face, *frequent smiles will increase sales.* And smiles can be felt over the phone—they are projected in the tone, pace, and loudness of the voice. Even if your employees will communicate mostly by phone, their smiles will strengthen relationships with suppliers and increase customer confidence—resulting in increased profits for you. You need to hire people who smile all the time, not just when they're particularly happy. Verbal communication goes only so far, but *a smile goes a mile.*

The second factor is the willingness to learn. I am much more concerned with potential employees' desire and ability to learn new skills than their prior employment or degrees. Unless your business involves, say, the manufacture of fighter-jet components (in which case you'd probably want to hire people with some experience in the aerospace industry), your first concern should be potential employees' personalities, not their résumés. If you find people with the right characteristics, you can always teach them sales, packaging, baking—whatever tasks their jobs will entail.

So, what are the right characteristics? From my experience and the experiences of the many master small-business people I know, five characteristics form the basic elements of a strong employee.

Positive attitude. Every business has plenty of problems and plenty of victories. Negative employees will focus only on the problems, driving themselves and you *crazy.* Team members with positive attitudes, in contrast, constantly trumpet small successes, creating an energetic, affirmative work environment. An employee's positive attitude is contagious; it inspires other workers, your suppliers, your customers, and you as well.

Reliability. If your team is properly configured, each member—every employee—should be a vital participant in the operation of your business. Therefore, if one person is excessively tardy or absent, your company will not be able to function properly. Further, one employee's failure to complete projects on schedule can disrupt the smooth operation of the company. You need reliable team members who arrive on time every day ready to fulfill their roles in your entrepreneurial expedition.

Consistency. You want people who will give you the same strong effort every day. People who are simply working to earn money will make an effort to impress you by expending extra effort when you're watching. But when you leave for a one-hour meeting or a one-month vacation, their productivity will decrease dramatically. In contrast, people who have a sense of pride in their work and an internal motivation to fulfill their potential will do excellent work all the time, whether you're watching or not. These are the employees you want.

Responsiveness. Imagine you own and run a book superstore. One of your employees, Franco, has the full-time task of stocking the shelves with new merchandise. As you observe him doing his work one day, you notice he is squeezing as many books as possible on every shelf, making it hard for customers to pull books out. So you tell him, "Franco, I really appreciate your hard work. Listen, I've noticed that the books are pretty tight on the shelves. I'd like you to leave some empty space on each shelf. I think the store will be more user-friendly."

"Absolutely," he says, and he goes back to work. The next day, you're strolling through the aisles, and you find Franco stocking the shelves. As you come closer, you see that he's stuffing the books in just as tightly as before. You have good reason to be annoyed. He acted as if he understood your request, but he simply ignored it. But Franco isn't trying to be rebellious. He just lacks the responsiveness characteristic. It's one thing for employees to be open to constructive feedback, both negative and positive, but entirely another thing to change their behavior as a result of it.

Deference. "I can't believe this," my entrepreneur friend said, calling me in the middle of the day. "I sent one of my employees a memo requesting that she see me at eleven. At ten-thirty she drops off a memo to my secretary. It says she won't meet me at eleven because I only gave her two hours notice of the meeting. She writes that she's too busy to see me without at least a day's notice."

"It sounds like she forgot who's the boss and who's the employee," I said. You want to foster a creative, comfortable, cooperative workplace, but your employees should accord you the respect you deserve as their employer. They don't need to genuflect when you enter the office in the morning, but they should understand that their main responsibility is to help you achieve your entrepreneurial dreams.

Back to the wise words of Henry David Thoreau: "Do not hire a man who does your work for money, but him who does it for love of it." Your ideal employees are people who are excited about accompanying you on an adventure, motivated not by their salaries but by the challenge of participating in an expedition into the jungle of entrepreneurship.

Selling Your Vision

You need to teach your employees about your product, the philosophy of your business, and most important, your vision of the company's future. You want to assimilate them into your business, helping them understand that they are team members working toward a common goal. After all, your employees are representatives of *you*, extensions of you in their dealings with customers and suppliers. Their actions create *your* public image.

Sell your employees on your vision to spark their enthusiasm and to get them excited about their roles in your expedition. When Mark Cohn launched Damark, a consumer-products catalog, he wasn't able to offer new employees much financial incentive. Instead, he had to sell them on the future of the company. Cohn says, "Back then, we were selling people on being on a rocket ship to the moon."[6] All he could promise them was a ticket to board a shuttle heading on an extraordinary mission. They could look forward to being a part of something big.

There is nothing wrong with expecting your employees to accept the prospect of future gain as a substitute for a higher initial salary. But when your company does thrive, you must make good on your promise to share the rewards.

Consider what happened to Henry Hudson, the seventeenth-century English adventurer. Hudson is famous both for his explorations and for having been the victim of a mutiny. In the spring of 1611, his crew rebelled after spending an incredibly harsh winter trapped in Hudson Bay. Hudson rationed supplies so sparsely that his men were forced to subsist on what little game they could hunt in the nearby woods.

Just three days after summer weather permitted them to sail out of the icy bay, the men suspected that Hudson had not been fair in allotting the supplies. According to the journal of Abacuck Prickett, one of the crew members, the men charged into Hudson's cabin and found "200 of biscuit cakes, a peck of meal, of beer to the quantity of a butt [roughly 125 gallons]." This was enough, in the eyes of the crew, to convict Hudson of treacherous misrepresentation, fraudulent subterfuge, chicanery, trickery, deceitfulness, duplicity, and a few other unmentionable wrongs. They placed him aboard a small dinghy—with no supplies—and sent him adrift in the huge icy bay. He was never seen or heard from again.[7]

It's unlikely that your employees would ever rise in mutiny, but don't underestimate the power of employees in sabotaging your business. Treat them fairly. Compensate them according to the significance of their role in your expedition's success. But compensation doesn't have to take the form of hard currency. Intangible benefits, like a friendly, comfortable working environment, are great motivators, too.

Establishing a Team-Oriented Workplace

I had a five o'clock flight to Los Angeles. I came home from the office at one o'clock to prepare some materials and pack. I had just returned from a long trip the night before, and when I went to the closet I found that I was out of clean shirts. So I called a local dry cleaner, and a peppy young woman answered, "Cleaners. Sue speaking." Not "Smith's Cleaners." Not "Magic Cleaners." Just "Cleaners." Sue probably didn't know the name of the business she worked for.

"Hello," I said, "I'm leaving for the airport in three hours, and I need some shirts laundered."

"OK," she said.

"Great! You can have them done in three hours?"

"No. They'll be ready by five tomorrow afternoon."

"I'll be Los Angeles tomorrow afternoon."

"Oh."

"Can you deliver them to Los Angeles?" I joked.

"They don't do that." She didn't like my humor.

"Do you have a rush-laundry service?" I asked.

"No. They don't do that."

"Maybe if I talk with 'they' I can convince them to do a rush job."

"What do you mean 'they'?"

"You said that they don't do rush laundry, so I just thought maybe I could convince 'they' to do my shirts fast."

"No, I mean *us*. We don't do rush laundry."

"Ah, now I understand. Well, thank you." And I hung up.

The way Sue talked, I was starting to think that "they" was an omnipotent being. She didn't understand that she, as a customer-service agent, is a representative and a team member of the business that employs her. She *is* the dry-cleaning company. She is *we*. This isn't merely a semantics problem—it's not just a question of which words to use. *The problem indicates a lack of togetherness, the absence of a team mentality*.

Really, Sue's use of "they" is not her fault. The owner of the dry-cleaning store had not fostered a venture adventure mentality among the staff. The employees were working for their $5 an hour, not out of any interest to participate in the growth of a small company.

Dwight Eisenhower said, "It is better to have one person working with you than having three people working for you." For your business to thrive, you have to cultivate a sense of ownership, participation, and pride among your employees. If they are committed to helping you build a strong company, they will be more productive, more effective, and most important, happier.

The second dry cleaner I called had an enthusiastic, team-oriented young woman working the phone. Not only did she promise to have the shirts done in three hours, she sensed I was busy, so she sent a van to fetch them from my house, and I picked them up on the way to the airport. My rush-laundry incident occurred about a year ago, and I've used that dry cleaner ever since.

I have developed five strategies you can implement to create a team-oriented work environment. When you hire new employees, brief them on the strategies you use to establish a feeling of *we-ness* (as opposed to *they-ness*) so they can assimilate quickly into your company.

Assign appropriate tasks. The members of your team will have specific strengths and weaknesses. Your challenge is first to accurately assess their abilities and then assign them appropriate tasks. You may hire someone with a strong creative background but find she has a special touch for sales. You would be wasting human resources if you had her doing creative work full time. The wise entrepreneur would slowly phase her out of creative work and into full-time sales. *Each person has a skill vital to the success of your expedition*, so you must discover what each person's primary skill actually is. It may not be the same skill for which you hired him or her. Then you have to assign responsibilities and duties that take advantage of what each person has to offer.

There are two kinds of employees: analyzers and technicians. Each behaves differently on the job. When analyzers walk down the hall of your office and find spilled coffee on the floor, they clean it up without deliberation. When technicians come across spilled coffee on the way to the copy machine, they step over it and continue to the copy room to efficiently complete their task.

Analyzers are capable of analyzing information and making a decision based on that analysis. They would quickly recognize the safety risk of spilled coffee in a hallway and act to eliminate the risk. On the other hand, technicians are focused and task-oriented. They set off to make copies. They didn't set off to clean up coffee puddles, so they don't.

You may be thinking that you'd like to have your team composed entirely of analyzers. Actually, the strongest small businesses have teams composed of both analyzers and technicians. The analyzers constantly evaluate the business and find ways to improve; the technicians complete tasks correctly and efficiently. Both kinds of team members are essential to your company. And in many cases, the skilled technicians demand higher salaries than do the analyzers.

Implement collective leadership. You can foster a sense of unity, equality, and mutual respect among your crew members by spreading leadership responsibility throughout the group. As your company grows, your employees will become responsible for performing a multitude of tasks, and you will not be able to supervise all of them personally. But even before you reach the point when you have to establish supervisory positions, allow the employees to feel they are in charge of a certain part of the business. Then each team member feels he or she has a voice in the leadership of the company.

Develop plans. First, make sure your employees thoroughly comprehend your vision. Next, develop pragmatic plans so they understand the importance of their roles in helping you turn your vision into reality. Plans also allow them to check their progress and evaluate their work. Developing plans is like showing your team members a map of the jungle of entrepreneurship and indicating your planned route so they know where you're going and how you're going to get there.

Create standards. From the start, notify your employees of the level of performance you expect from them. You may have the same standards for all employees, such as selling fifty sets of tires a month, or you may have different standards for each employee depending on the position. Your team members will find it much easier to participate in your venture adventure when they know from the beginning what you expect from them. When they know what they're striving for, they can take steps to meet or exceed the standards.

Encourage continual self-evaluation. Employees should constantly evaluate their work and the progress of the team as a whole. Encourage them to continually review the plans and the standards you've created for them so they can choose to continue their present efforts or change their actions to better work toward your vision. Self-evaluation creates a greater sense of unity and company pride among employees.

Establishing a comfortable, team-oriented work environment is only the beginning. As your business grows and changes, one of your primary responsibilities as the leader of the entrepreneurial expedition is to maintain the atmosphere you created at the launch of the venture. Your role is critical. Your attitude—your enthusiasm and excitement—sets the tone of the business.

You may or may not need to assemble a crew from the outset of your venture adventure. Most entrepreneurs begin small, traveling alone. As their businesses grow, they assemble a staff. I've seen solo entrepreneurs hire their first employees as soon as *two weeks* after launching their companies, because their businesses take off much faster than they had expected. And I know other entrepreneurs who have been running extremely profitable one-person businesses for decades. The number of people you employ does not determine your level of success in business. *Your happiness and your feeling of fulfillment are the indicators of achievement.*

Finding ideal partners and assembling an expeditionary team are challenging tasks, but if performed correctly they form the foundation of a strong, thriving business. Allow your team members to participate fully in the adventure—to experience the thrill—and they will serve you with honesty, loyalty, and productivity. But remember that you are the heart of the business: you hire, you train, you maintain. The performance of your expeditionary force is ultimately your responsibility.

Choose your expeditionary team members carefully,
for they are the people with whom you'll be working
every day to turn your vision into reality.

PART **V**

On the

Expedition

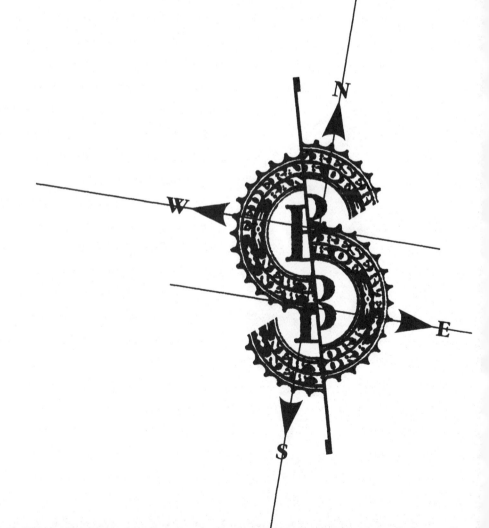

Introduction to Part V

Launching your venture adventure is only half the challenge. The other half is running your business successfully—increasing sales and profits, creating happy customers, retaining employees, and perhaps most important, maintaining your excitement and enjoyment.

When you do "good" business—treat clients and employees well, invest in the community, and build your network—your business will grow naturally. A happy customer base is like a snowball. The first year you have 1,000 customers, the second year 1,500, the third year 2,000, and so on. Good business results in increased sales without any further effort from you. But when you take *action* to grow your business, your sales increases will be substantially higher.

Yet what good is more money if you and your employees aren't having fun? A positive work environment, strong relationships with suppliers and customers, and community involvement all contribute to your enjoyment. By implementing proven strategies *on the expedition*, you can be sure you'll have a great time while growing your company. Your business should bring you fulfillment and income for many years.

You are not here merely to make a living. You are here in order to enable the world to live more amply, with greater vision, with a finer spirit of hope and achievement.

Woodrow Wilson (1856–1924)
Twenty-eighth president of the United States

As I write these words, I am sitting in Venice, Italy, where I am participating in a conference on world conflicts at the invitation of the Elie Wiesel Foundation for Humanity. I have heard young people from regions ravaged by war, famine, and ethnic strife describe their experiences. Their stories have had a significant impact on my outlook. I realize that those of us who have crafted enjoyable, comfortable lifestyles for ourselves are a small minority. Most people on planet Earth, the majority of our fellow human beings, have difficult lives.

As a venture adventurer, you will become a recipient of the benefits of a capitalistic society. Not only will you enjoy every day of your life, you will be generously compensated as well. But what really differentiates you from other people is that as a successful entrepreneur, you have the ability to truly change lives. *The free-enterprise system creates wealth.* Use your wealth, your influence, and your voice to end suffering, not just because it gives you a sense of fulfillment, but because as a rational, intelligent being you have a moral responsibility to help others.

The promise of entrepreneurship is *the betterment of society*—increasing the quality of life through the advancement of innovative goods and services, creation of employment opportunities, and promotion of a healthy, ethical business community. As an entrepreneur, *you have the capability to help build a better society*, whether on a local, national, or international level.

You *can* be conscious of the importance of your role in society, unlike many of the adventurers I have presented in this book. Although explorers like Livingstone and Columbus are to be admired for many of their characteristics, such as their courage, decisiveness, and self-confidence, they should not be revered as models of ethical behavior.

After all, the world's foremost explorers and adventurers were also the leading proponents of Western colonization. Their efforts to travel the world in search of knowledge and wealth represent a collective European ambition to conquer other lands and subdue other peoples. The adventurers did not strive to foster a healthy, international economic system of mutually beneficial trade. Fueled by patriotic and religious fervor, and justified by a false sense of intellectual and moral superiority, they ventured forth on avaricious quests for power, fame, and wealth.

On his first voyage to the New World, Columbus claimed possession of the land, its natural resources, and its people. As tangible evidence of his conquest, he returned to Spain with about two dozen Native Americans—gifts to the Spanish royalty. Even Livingstone, who in missionary travels in South Africa aimed to spread religion and help abolish the slave trade, assumed that African culture and religion was somehow inferior to European models.

Responsibilities

Fortunately, you have the opportunity to approach your travels in the jungle of entrepreneurship with a much more socially conscious attitude. *As an entrepreneur, as the owner of a one-person or a thousand-person company, you play a major role in shaping society.* Business leader and writer Paul Hawken, in his book *The Ecology of Commerce*, writes that businesses, "because they are the dominant institution on the planet, must squarely address the social and environmental problems that afflict humankind."[1] Businesspeople have a greater capability to solve social problems than any other collective entity, because together they employ more people, control more money, and have a wider geographical distribution than any government, charitable, or humanitarian organization. As an entrepreneur, you have three major responsibilities.

Make a profit. If you don't make money, you can't stay open. And if you can't stay open, you won't have the ability to use your business to improve society. Profits allow you to invest in your community and support humanitarian efforts. If your furniture store is reporting monthly losses of $10,000, surely you're not going to sponsor an airlift of food to a starved area of the globe. However, if you first concentrate on building a thriving business, then you can afford to expend some energy and money on socially responsible activities.

Give back to the community a portion of what you take. Some entrepreneurs choose to donate a portion of their profits to charities and humanitarian organizations. Rabbi Wayne Dosick, author of *The Business Bible*, suggests that you give 10 percent. "From every dollar you make, give a dime to a person or to a cause that needs your help."[2] You don't have to be a Rockefeller to become a philanthropist. Whatever you can afford to give makes a difference.

Wayne Embrey, author of *Doing Well While Doing Good* and owner of the World Villages Coffee Company, walks his talk. A former consultant to giant corporations such as Ashland Oil, General Motors, and IBM, Embrey has preached social responsibility in business for years. Recently, he opened a coffeehouse and donated a portion of its proceeds to charitable causes. Within five months after opening, World Villages donated $25,000 to the Red Cross. Embrey expects its newly opened second store to generate close to $100,000 annually for local charities.

Whether you donate your time and effort, your money, or perhaps your products or services, giving to charitable causes is not a wholly selfless act. Altruism need not be the sole purpose of your philanthropy. *Giving is, in the long run, good for your business.* In an interview with *The Arizona Republic*, Embrey explained that one of the motivations for social responsibility is "the competitive reality. It isn't about the esoteric and ethereal feature of being able to save the planet."[3] Embrey realizes that being socially conscious simply makes good business sense.

Capitalism is competitive, and to thrive you have to find new advantages in the marketplace. Social responsibility can give you an advantage. Your social action can distinguish you from your competitors. Giving to the community creates consumer awareness of your company, subsequently increasing your sales. In today's economy, customers respect companies that participate in social amelioration. Your involvement in your city, your nation, or other regions of the world will increase and solidify your customer base.

Support a stable, cooperative business ecosystem. In a larger context, your company is part of an intricate network of businesses in the jungle of entrepreneurship. Just as animals are dependent on one another to sustain themselves in the natural environment, entrepreneurs are dependent on one another in the world of business. A variety of small birds sit in and around the mouths of alligators. The alligator allows the birds to nibble the tiny organisms that live on its teeth. They have a symbiotic, harmonious relationship. The birds get dinner and the alligators get free dental work.

Livingstone found it remarkable "how organizations the most dissimilar depend on each other for their perpetuation."[4] And so it is in business. If you run a hardware store, for example, to maintain a healthy existence you depend on other businesses, and many other businesses depend on you. You provide a service for all the companies that make hammers, screwdrivers, and saws by selling their products for them. You also support the shipping companies that deliver goods to your store. At the same time, you depend on plumbers, electricians, and mechanics to buy your products. When their businesses do well, your business does well.

Your hardware store is a participant in a fragile business ecosystem. If one part of the ecosystem fails, everyone suffers. If your major electric-cord supplier goes out of business, your revenues decrease, and your customers have trouble running their businesses. Selfish, maniacal entrepreneurs who pillage the jungle of business don't realize that they are hurting their potential for long-term success.

Even your competitors are important participants in the ecosystem. Inexperienced entrepreneurs think business is about crushing the competition, about putting them out of business. But competition is what fuels a free-enterprise economy. Competition creates demand, forces product improvements, and produces better customer service. In the world's $21 trillion economy, there's plenty of room for everyone. Anyone with the drive and the proper mentality can carve out plenty of profits in the jungle of entrepreneurship.

Treating People Well

Rabbi Dosick, in *The Business Bible*, tells a great story about an incident at an airport ticket counter. A customer at the counter was very upset and was berating the clerk. He was yelling, throwing his hands in the air, and calling the clerk names. But the clerk did not get upset. She kept saying, "Yes, sir. I understand."

After the angry customer finally threw up his hands one last time and left, the next person in line, who had watched the whole interaction, said to the clerk, "That guy was obnoxious. How did you just absorb all those insults without getting furious?"

And the clerk responded, "Oh, it's all right, you see, because that man is going to Cleveland. But his luggage is going to Singapore."[5]

In business, you deal with dozens of people every day, every one of whom could send your luggage to Singapore. Being aggressive or belligerent will only make your life more difficult. By treating people fairly, you will strengthen your relationships with customers and suppliers, eventually increasing your sales and profits. But more important, *by treating people with dignity and respect, you're making a small step toward establishing a kinder, more compassionate society.*

Profits and principles can, in fact, exist simultaneously. Aside from your moral obligation to assist fellow human beings, your positive social action— whether donating money to humanitarian causes or simply treating a customer well—gives you a sense of personal fulfillment and helps your business in the long run. Tread lightly in the jungle of entrepreneurship so as not to disturb the magnificent, fragile business ecosystem.

Amend the behavior of previous adventurers
by using your power as an entrepreneur
to improve the quality of life for all world citizens.

*Not a having and a
resting, but a growing and
a becoming is the character
of perfection as culture
conceives it.*

Matthew Arnold (1822–1888)
English poet

Bernard Marcus and Arthur Blank were executives of Handy Dan, a small chain of home-improvement stores owned by Daylin Corporation. In 1979, the head of Daylin was sufficiently annoyed with the brazen executives to fire them. The newly unemployed Marcus and Blank opted to abandon the corporate world and launch a venture adventure. They wanted to use their experience in the home-improvement-products industry, but they weren't going to open a hardware store. They had a much bigger vision.

The same year they were fired, they opened their first retail business, a warehouse filled with home-improvement supplies. Boasting rock-bottom prices and top-notch service, the business boomed, and within one year the duo opened four more stores. But Marcus and Blank were not content yet. They wanted to expand, to become the biggest in the business. They focused on growth, and today their little business has 359 stores and $12.5 billion in revenues. They call it Home Depot.[1]

Every business goes through two major stages: development and growth. The development stage—the birth of the business idea and the launching of the company—can take as little as a few days, as in the case of, say, an ice-cream stand, or as long as ten years for a large retail store or restaurant. The growth stage begins as soon as the company becomes stable, self-reliant, and profitable. In growing, companies attempt to increase revenues and profits, expand into subsidiary businesses, enter new geographical territories, and increase distribution. Growth is the process of becoming larger, whether in sales, number of employees, or locations.

Some believe that entrepreneurship is about starting companies and that the most exciting part of business is the development stage—coming up with the idea and creating a company. But the growth stage is just as much fun and is even more challenging.

The Power of Leverage

Because you are the heart of your company, the leader of your entrepreneurial expedition, you have to leverage your knowledge and your energy. Alone, you will go only so far. However, with the help of a skilled, carefully chosen team, you can turn a small business into a thriving, growing company. The secret? *You spend a large part of your time concentrating on new ideas for improvement and expansion. You let your employees take care of the daily operation and implement your growth ideas.*

Consider how Thomas and Mary Helen Falls grew Falls Janitorial Inc. from a husband-and-wife cleaning team into a multimillion-dollar service business. They spent $300 for their first floor-buffing machine and set to work scrubbing and mopping a local industrial building. After forty days of hard work, word of mouth brought them their second customer. As more and more customers flocked to Falls Janitorial, they were able to hire a few employees, then a few more, then a lot more, until their employees did all the cleaning for them.

Hiring employees allowed them to leverage their efforts and focus on growing the business. "When I first hired employees, it freed me up to make a lot of phone calls," Thomas Falls told me. He learned quickly that his time was much better spent finding new customers than mopping floors. Today, many phone calls later, Falls Janitorial Inc. has 350 employees in three southern states.[2]

You may experience a feeling of separation, a sense of insecurity in handing over to your employees the day-to-day tasks of your business—whether cooking pizzas, doing oil changes, or consulting with physicians. But the only way to grow your company is to spend your time working *on* the business, not *in* the business.

Provide High-Quality Goods and Services

The most proven way to ensure continued success is to produce the *best*—not one of the best, but *the best*—quality goods and services on the market. My father relayed to me something his father told him many times. "America is an incredible country," my grandfather said. "If you are the best at what you do, you will live well. *If you can kick a can down the street better than anyone else, you will succeed in America.*"

When you offer the best product on the market, customers will come to you, and they will stay with you. If your customers are happy with the way they are treated, they'll continue to patronize your business again and again.

One of the common causes of business failure is the absence of what I call the *lifelong-customer objective.*

Inexperienced entrepreneurs often try to make as much money as they can from every sale. The advantage: they make some solid profits for a short time. The problem: most of their customers never patronize their business again. *Your goal in customer service is to make every customer a lifelong customer.*

Just imagine: You serve ten new customers every day in your small sandwich shop, San Francisco Sandwiches. And every customer is totally satisfied with your product and your service and plans to return at least once a week for a sandwich. At the end of week one you have seventy happy customers. The next week, you serve the seventy happy customers from week one and seventy new customers, all of whom are thrilled with your delicious gourmet sandwiches and your enthusiastic employees. During week three, you serve the 140 happy customers from weeks one and two and seventy new customers. By the end of your first year in business, assuming you continue to advertise enough to bring in seventy new customers every week, you'd be serving about 3,600 sandwiches every day. By the end of year two, you'd be serving 7,200 sandwiches every day, making your one-location San Francisco Sandwiches about an $8 million yearly business.

Now, of course, in reality not every customer you serve will return every week for the rest of his or her life, and to serve 7,200 sandwiches a day you'd have to a 100,000-square-foot kitchen. But the idea of the lifelong-customer objective is that by providing the best product or service available anywhere, people will remain customers for a long, long time.

Value Creates Satisfaction

Dining in Italy makes me uncomfortable. Even though the food is, in my opinion, the best in the world, Italian restaurateurs' business strategies bother me. From the minute I walk into their restaurants, whether in big cities like Milan, Florence, and Rome or in smaller towns like Poggibonsi and Orvieto, I feel as though they're much more interested in taking my money than in providing me with an enjoyable dining experience. Most restaurants charge a *coperto*, a cover charge. So before you even put your napkin on your lap, they've begun charging you.

And it gets worse! The first course of the meal, the *primi piatti*, usually consists of a portion of pasta. In the United States, we're used to receiving a heaping pile of spaghetti, but the *primi piatti* is so small you can count the number of pasta strands on your plate. I could accept the small portion, because Italian pasta is exceedingly more tasty than anything I've had here. But the price for the appetizer is exorbitant—roughly what you might expect to pay for an entrée. Keep in mind, this is not the Four Seasons. It's just a neighborhood Italian restaurant, and the bill is topping $20 a person as we wipe our lips after the appetizer.

The main course arrives. The waiter triumphantly places it in front of me as if it were the English crown. Since the delicious but meager *primi piatti*, I've been imagining my fish entrée: a glorious, succulent filet of fish surrounded by delicate roasted potatoes and perhaps some vegetables marinated in the local olive oil. I look at my plate. Staring back at me is a scrawny little fish—head, tail, and all—definitely no longer than six inches. That's it. There's nothing else on the plate—just my pathetic little $20 amphibious friend. So go my Italian dining experiences.

I shouldn't be too tough on the Italian restaurants, because the culture is quite different from ours. But what bothers me is that the restaurant owners don't understand the importance of making customers feel that they've received value. Customer satisfaction is the key to a profitable, long-lasting business. Here's the secret to creating happy customers that I share in my seminars: *Satisfied customers feel they have received more from you than you have received from them.* Think about it and I am certain you'll agree it makes sense.

Happy customers are like walking billboards, living advertisements for your business. If you provide a great product with friendly service, your customers will not only continue to patronize your business, but they will spread the news about your business to more and more people.

In fact, the level of service that businesses provide for their customers is a much more important growth factor than most entrepreneurs realize. I read a report recently stating that *price is only the fourth most influential force that motivates customers to patronize a business.* Service, reputation, and ease of access are higher on the list. People are much more interested in patronizing a business with friendly employees, a solid reputation, and easy purchasing procedures than in chasing around for the best price.

As I grow and improve my businesses, I encourage the *Every-Customer-Counts Mentality* (ECCM). Imagine that you own Wild Wear, a clothing mail-order company. You send out one hundred packages on a certain day. If one of those packages happened to contain the wrong product, most business owners wouldn't be too concerned. In fact, they'd probably be quite happy with a 99 percent rate of accuracy.

But that one mistake is *one mistake too many for the ECCM-minded entrepreneur!* The customer who receives the bad package is dissatisfied with your service. She doesn't know about the ninety-nine correct packages; she sees only the mistake. From her vantage point, Wild Wear is 100 percent sloppy! Every customer counts, so strive for 100 percent accuracy in all aspects of your business.

Take Time to Think

Robert E. Peary, in recounting his expedition to the North Pole, said, "The rush of getting on board my Eskimos and dogs, re-stowing the ship and fighting the ice, had left me no time for a thought beyond the demands of each hour."[3] Although I haven't been anywhere near the North Pole, I know the feeling.

The daily demands of an entrepreneurial expedition can keep you so busy that you never stop to think about the more conceptual issues: the direction in which you're headed, the progress you're making, your company's potential for growth, and your relationships with customers and suppliers. You can easily become so embroiled in negotiating, selling, and servicing that you neglect the most important function of the entrepreneur in a venture adventure—thinking.

I like traveling to distant places, like the Greek islands, because I can think freely. I am so far away from my offices that I begin to forget the daily intricacies of my companies. Instead, as I sip cold orange juice and stare out at the stunning green-blue Mediterranean, I can dream of brilliant new directions for my companies, innovative strategies for improvement, fresh advertising campaigns, product concepts, and new business ideas. *Every time I take a month, a week, or even a day to get away and think, to reflect, I return with new insights that increase my profits and my enjoyment.*

Thor Heyerdahl, captain of the *Kon Tiki*, explained, "Weather permitting, we often got into our rubber float, two or three at a time, and took a 'vacation' from our sturdy log raft to study our craft from a distance."[4] Sitting on their raft, Heyerdahl and his crew couldn't accurately examine its structure, condition, and appearance. Only by looking at it from a distance could they assess any damage or spot potential points for improvement.

Similarly, sitting in your office, you can't properly examine your business. Unlike Heyerdahl's "vacations" from his raft, walking across the street and staring at the building that houses your company won't help you much. You have to *mentally* study your business from a distance. Only then can you examine *objectively* the various parts of your entrepreneurial expedition—your location, products, customer service, advertising, office configuration, employees, and public image—to find areas needing refinement or improvement.

Keeping an expedition journal is another strategy for encouraging improvement and growth. Every day, thousands of small reflections pass through our minds, but they occur so often and so rapidly that we think about each for just a few seconds before moving on to the next. In fact, small thoughts pass through our heads so quickly that there is no way we can remember them unless we record them. Of course, we don't want to write down everything that passes through our minds, but it's valuable to record *learnings, observations, strategies, and hopes.*

Your expedition journal doesn't have to resemble a novel. I know many entrepreneurs who jot down phrases, words, and sentence fragments throughout the day. If you come up with an especially interesting idea, you may wish to describe it in a paragraph so you don't forget it, but otherwise you can use just a few words. Later, maybe the following day or maybe a year later, you can review your thoughts. By keeping a journal and reading it frequently, you'll become an exceptional entrepreneur because you'll always have your collected learnings fresh in your head.

Patrick Henry proclaimed, "I have but one lamp by which my feet are guided, and that is the lamp of experience." In business, as in life, you have one educational experience after another, but you have a selective memory. You retain only a small portion of your ideas and learnings unless you record your significant thoughts and experiences in an expedition journal. Review your notes regularly, and your lamp of experience, shining bright, will lead you to unfound treasures in the jungle of entrepreneurship.

Invest in Your Growth

One of the biggest impediments to growth is entrepreneurs' unwillingness to finance it. As illogical as it may sound, many business owners never expand their operations because they are reluctant to invest in new equipment, locations, or employees. A clothing-store owner may purchase $10,000 worth of sweaters to sell during the winter season but stubbornly refuses to purchase a flashy $2,000 sign that will bring more customers into the store. More customers mean more profits, but the entrepreneur is unwilling to invest in anything but inventory. This behavior is irrational, but it's common. *In growing a business, you have to spend money to make money.*

Previously, I discussed the importance of maintaining a strong cash flow in order to finance growth and expansion. Here are a few ways you can use that cash to grow your business.

Follow up on contacts. When you meet promising contacts at a conference, on an airplane, or at a cocktail party, follow up with calls, letters, packages, and even trips. The wider your network of customers, suppliers, journalists, sales reps, wholesalers, dealers, and even competitors, the more potential for growth your company has. Don't hesitate to spend the money to take someone to lunch or dinner. If the contact lives in another state or, depending on your industry, another country, investing in a trip often pays great dividends. One funny thing about contacts: you have to pursue about twenty to find one who has the true potential to multiply your revenues.

Buy books and magazine subscriptions. Books on marketing, sales, advertising, customer service, hiring, firing, motivation, negotiating, inventing, distributing, and fostering creativity are abundant. Read them. Use them. Subscribe to many magazines and newsletters. They will keep you aware of the trends within your industry and, more important, give you ideas for new growth avenues for your company. Leading business and industry publications feature trailblazing companies. Read the publications carefully, and you will find many innovations you can implement in your business.

Attend conventions. Yes, entry fees, airfare, hotels, and food do add up fast, but the knowledge and contacts you bring back from conventions are well worth the money spent. You find new customers, new suppliers, new products, and new ways to sell the products you already offer.

Take advantage of technology. We live in a wild time. Technology is advancing at an exponential rate—each month we see double or triple the number of developments that occurred during the previous month. Such rapid change can seem a little overwhelming, but technological advancements are bringing great benefits for entrepreneurs. Technology can help you increase productivity, output, and sales. *Every technology purchase I have authorized for my companies, no matter how seemingly extravagant at the time, has brought at least $100 in benefit for every dollar it cost.* A $1,000 item results in more than $100,000 in increased sales.

Computers, if installed and used properly, can singlehandedly turn a small business into a thriving business. During crazy days at any of my companies, I usually order pizzas for everyone. Managerial secret: Good pizzas have a magical effect on energy and morale. I always call the same pizza place—they've had the best pizza for a long time. About a year ago, they installed an amazing computer system. When I called in the past, they took my name, company name, address, phone number, directions, and the pizzas

I wanted. At some point, they logged all that information into their computer database.

Now I call and a friendly operator answers, "Thank you for calling Pisa Pizza! Is this Daryl Bernstein?" Yes, *she already knows my name when she picks up the phone.* The computer is hooked up to a caller-identification service available through the local phone company. I confirm that I am, she hits a key, and instantly she has on her screen my office address and directions to get there. Here's the best part: she even knows what pizzas I last ordered, and she asks if I enjoyed them. Then, if I choose, I can place the same order again without describing all the pizzas. The whole call lasts about twenty seconds, compared with two or three minutes before the computers. The technology saves time for both of us, provides me with more personalized customer service, and allows the pizza people to develop an incredible customer database for promotions. I can't attribute all their success to their computer system, but recently these pizza entrepreneurs opened a slew of new locations, one after another, more than I can count. Using advanced technology, this company is growing like mad in an area already saturated with big corporate-owned pizza chains.

In 1958, William R. Anderson piloted the nuclear-powered submarine *Nautilus* underneath the Arctic ice cap and reached the North Pole nearly fifty years after Robert Peary achieved distinction by traveling there overland with Eskimos and sled dogs. As the submarine glided smoothly through the icy waters far beneath the rugged glaciers, one of Anderson's crew, pipe in hand and holding a cup of coffee, remarked, "Boy, this is the way to explore . . . fresh air all day long, a warm boat; I'd hate to walk across these ice fields up there to the Pole the way Admiral Peary did it."[5] Modern technology certainly has its advantages!

Why spend a long time struggling to reach your North Pole when an investment in advanced technology can help you reach your destination quickly with comfort and ease? Many people refuse to buy computers, phone systems, and other pieces of technology because, they say, these items are too expensive and they will be outdated too soon. Absolutely correct. Technology is quite costly, and it is rather annoying to purchase upgrades frequently. Still, I never hesitate to spend money on new advancements in technology, because every piece of equipment I've purchased has, directly or indirectly, resulted in increased sales. The pizza store demonstrates that technology can help any business grow.

Invest in research and development. After giving a speech near Los Angeles, I had an afternoon free and wandered around the Laguna Beach area. I spotted a small store with a lot of people both inside and milling around the window, so I crossed the street and went in. I quickly understood why the store was full. It was filled with a variety of modern, attractive, functional household items. As I roamed the store, I found at least ten items I was interested in buying for my home or for gifts for employees, family, and friends. The cash register was ringing like crazy, and the owner, working by herself, was having a great time. When the other customers had paid and left and the store was quieter, I picked out several items—a tall compact-disc stand, a pair of artistic candlesticks, and a bizarre glass-and-rock candy dish—and brought them to the counter.

"Looks like business is good," I said.

"It's amazing," she said. "I've been open for two years, and it hasn't slowed down for a day."

"Your products are so unique," I said, "you'd make a fortune if you opened stores in other tourist areas, like the waterfront in San Francisco, any of the beach towns in Florida, or South Street Seaport in Boston. I know your store would be packed in Scottsdale, where I live."

"I've thought about it," she said, "but I just don't know if there'd be enough traffic in other places."

"There's only one way to find out," I said. "Jump on a plane and visit some other cities. See if you can find a retail space with as much traffic as you have here. I've found with my companies that investments in R and D always pay off."

She thanked me for the advice, went into the back of the store, and returned with a tiny oak statue of a tree. She gave it to me for, as she said, "making me realize I should spend a little of the money I'm earning to grow my business."

Natural Growth Patterns

While growing, your business will exhibit some erratic behavior. As you begin to make changes in your operation—adding employees, opening new locations, or purchasing more equipment—your profits will drop before they rise. *It's normal for profits to go down before going up*, so don't become alarmed when this happens.

Imagine the case of Pierre, founder and proud owner of Pie in the Sky Inc., a commercial bakery. During the past year, Pierre has increased his business dramatically, opening new accounts with two large grocery stores, many restaurants, and a few coffeehouses. He's now working sixteen hours a day, by himself, to turn out one hundred pies daily. He's refined the baking process to a science, and he simply cannot bake any more pies each day. One hundred is the maximum.

The owner of a large restaurant hears about the fresh, natural ingredients in Pie in the Sky's pies, and she calls Pierre. She would like to purchase ten pies a day, she says. Pierre is thrilled with the added business, but he has a problem. He simply cannot bake another pie without expanding his operation. So while sipping coffee and indulging in a piece of his now-famous Very Berry pie, he mulls over the situation and decides that he really wants to grow his business. All his machines—mixers, ovens, and packaging systems—sit dormant for eight hours every night, so Pierre decides to hire an employee to bake during the time he sleeps.

While baking one hundred pies by himself, Pierre was earning $300 per day—exactly $3 profit per pie. Pierre has agreed to pay his new employee, Sam, $75 per eight-hour shift. So Sam begins working during Pierre's off-hours, and production is increased to 110 pies each day. Pierre's profit on the pies increases to $330 per day. But after he pays Sam, he goes home with only $255, or $45 less than what he was making before he began to grow his business!

This is the point at which many entrepreneurs decide that growth is a bad idea. A decrease in profits is not their idea of growth, so they fire the new employee and scale back to their original output level.

But Pierre has read this book, and he understands that profits go down before going up. He's determined to grow his business. Just as he can bake one hundred pies in sixteen hours, his employee soon becomes skilled and can bake fifty pies during his eight-hour shift. So Pie in the Sky Inc. now has a production capacity of 150 pies. Pierre spends some time on the phone calling grocery stores and restaurants. Because practically everyone has heard about his delicious pies, he quickly signs up several new customers who together request forty pies a day. So after a short growth effort, Pierre's profits are up to $375: $450 of profit on the 150 pies minus Sam's salary. In just a few weeks, Pierre has increased his daily profit 25 percent.

Like Pie in the Sky Inc., your business will experience a decrease in profits each time you take action to grow, whether hiring a new employee, buying equipment, launching an ad campaign, or opening another location. As Pierre demonstrated, this is a natural pattern of growth. Maintain your commitment to the growth process and you'll soon begin to see your profits head north.

Lions on the Hunt

Livingstone wrote, "Where game is abundant, lions may be expected in proportion."[6] When your business begins to thrive, you'll attract competition. You'll likely become annoyed at the audacity of your rivals, but remember that the United States has a *free*-enterprise system. Other businesses have the right to pursue a treasure in the jungle of entrepreneurship just as you do.

At that point, you'll need to make a distinction among your competitors. You must determine which are preparing to attack and which are merely scouting the territory for leftovers.

Livingstone noted further, "There is, it must be admitted, a considerable distinction between the singing noise of a lion when full and his deep gruff growl when hungry."[7] Some competitors will have no intent to harm you—they'll simply be looking for their own niche. Others, however, will rush into your territory quite aggressively, intent on wresting from you a significant portion of the market. These are the ones you have to keep an eye on.

To maintain the steady growth of your business, you'll need to acknowledge the presence of your competitors. As I discussed previously, the best defensive strategy is to refine *your* business. Improve your product, sharpen your service, and promote the positive aspects of your company. Competition is a good sign, an indication that your market is ripe for growth. Bolster your growth efforts, and you'll scare most competitors out of your territory.

Leverage your knowledge, intuition, and energy by investing in employees. Make sure your company is providing the highest-quality goods and services possible. Establish prices that help customers feel they are receiving more from you than you are receiving from them. Devote time to examining your business from an external viewpoint. Get away and think. Use technology to your advantage, and spend money on research and development. Recognize the natural growth process, and expect competition.

Turning a small business into a thriving business is a challenge, an exciting component of your venture adventure. You don't have to envision 359 locations and multibillions in revenues as a destination. Fifty more pies may be your growth goal. Either way, successful growth depends on your commitment to the process. Expansion efforts are never smooth, but that's why the growth stage is so challenging. You have to maintain your confidence in your vision and your determination to reach it.

> ***Launching a business can make you money.***
> ***Growing a business can make you rich.***

CHAPTER **25** Maintaining the
Adventure Mentality

> *You cannot consistently*
> *perform in a manner which*
> *is inconsistent with the way*
> *you see yourself.*

Zig Ziglar
Speaker and author

In this book I have described the characteristics, success strategies, and thought processes of successful entrepreneurs and explorers alike. I have attempted to convey the energy and excitement that accompany the entrepreneurial lifestyle. I have portrayed a new way of thinking about business, the way *I* think about business.

By now I hope you are confident in your ability to survive and thrive in the jungle of entrepreneurship. But your work isn't finished when you put down this book. At this point, in fact, your adventure has just begun.

Maintaining the adventure mentality as you venture into the business world is imperative to your success. Your positive emotion and energy soon will begin to dissipate. Your challenge is to preserve the adventurous, enthusiastic state of mind you've developed while reading this book. *Envisioning yourself as an adventure entrepreneur, not just an entrepreneur, will have a significant impact on your performance.*

By conveying the tales of the world's most accomplished entrepreneurs and explorers, I have tried to create a link between business and adventure. As you launch and run your company, continue to refer to the adventure analogy; I believe it provides the most accurate representation of the true spirit of entrepreneurship.

Compare your business challenges to adventure challenges. For example, suppose you're faced with a challenge, like the appearance of a new print shop down the block. Imagine how as an adventurer you might handle a similar situation. You're on safari on the African plains and a group of gruff and hungry lions pace about in the distance. Should you level your gun and begin shooting, that is, launch an all-out advertising campaign to maintain your hold on the market? Or should you keep your distance and move around the lions, confident that they represent no threat to your stronghold on the market? Placing the day-to-day challenges of your business into the context of an adventure will help you recall the pertinent lessons from this book.

Take time to reflect on the adventure stories you find most poignant, meaningful, or motivational. Review the stories as well as the lessons they represent. You may enjoy the myth of Timbuktu and the lesson it teaches about savoring the small pleasures of your adventure. Or you may appreciate the story of the great Ross Ice Barrier and the importance of confronting obstacles with courage and determination. Stories bring learnings to life, so one of the best ways to keep your collected knowledge alive is to ponder frequently stories that have meaning for you.

You can motivate yourself by mentally repeating key phrases—what the media call "sound bites"—that you find in your reading. This practice helps you to focus your attention on the *key aspects* of your venture adventure. Picture an author, speaker, entrepreneur, or adventurer speaking directly to you, using a vivid phrase applicable to your situation at the moment.

Even better still, write down those key phrases and motivational sayings. I have them on scraps of paper scattered on my desktop and in my desk drawers. Write them in the margins of your paperwork. Consider recording your favorite lines on posters that you can hang in your store or office. *When you put those statements on paper, they become not only visual reminders but tangible evidence of your commitment to realizing your dreams.*

You can sustain the excitement of the adventure mentality by continuing to read. Bookstores are full of good books on business and motivation. I strongly suggest you pick up a few of the adventure books I've mentioned. The journals of Livingstone and Peary are more exciting than most novels. Find out first-hand how the members of the *Kon Tiki* raft expedition and other explorers persevered and reached their destinations. Discover how much the world's greatest explorers and adventurers have in common with today's most successful entrepreneurs. Use their stories of daring adventure to keep yourself mentally prepared to meet the challenges of the business world.

While you're traveling in the jungle of entrepreneurship, keep your vision in the forefront of your mind. Think about it. Improve it. Revise it. Frequently examine the direction in which you're heading and evaluate the progress you've made. Identify the pleasures you're experiencing in running your business. *Remember that you are not just an entrepreneur; you are an adventure entrepreneur.*

In sum, the characteristics of adventure entrepreneurs, the principles of travel in the jungle, and the strategies of successful expedition leadership form a comprehensive *adventure mentality*. They describe a state of mind that helps you survive and thrive in the jungle of entrepreneurship and the jungle of life.

Your adventure mentality may begin to dissipate soon after you put this book down. To compensate for this inevitable lapse in mental stamina, I have summarized the adventure mentality in "The Eight Core Beliefs of the Adventure Entrepreneur" on pages 195 and 196. These beliefs represent the general ideas I present in this book, and they capture the spirit of adventure entrepreneurship as I describe it.

Periodically refer to these beliefs as you launch and grow your business. Read them with enthusiasm, conviction, and passion. They will motivate you, rejuvenate you, and refresh your adventure mentality.

Later in your business adventure, when you review the core beliefs, you may find you cannot fully endorse all of them. For instance, in reading belief number five, "*I am a cautious, alert traveler*," you may say to yourself, "No, I'm not cautious anymore. In fact, I've been acting quite impulsively lately. I haven't been carefully calculating my risks." To amend the gap in your adventure mentality, refer to passages in the book that may help you deliberate and assess risk. The eight beliefs are helpful as a self-test to quickly analyze your perspective on business at the moment. As you read through them, if you believe you are conducting your venture adventure in a way that fulfills every statement, you can be confident your adventure mentality is intact. *Maintain the adventure mentality throughout your venture adventure and you will make big money, change lives, and love every minute of it.*

In using the adventure metaphor, I have attempted to convey the dynamism, the challenge, the intensity of starting and running a business. My purpose in writing *The Venture Adventure* has been to enable you to use entrepreneurship to enrich all aspects of your life. Entrepreneurship is not a way to make a living. *It is a way of living.*

Aristotle said, "For the things we have to learn before we can do them, we learn by doing them." You have studied the insights of those who have traveled before you. Now you are ready to embark. I wish you an enjoyable, fulfilling, and rewarding adventure.

With regard and admiration,

Daryl Bernstein

1
I am an entrepreneur because I love the adventure of business.

I view money as a means to achieving fulfillment and improving the lives of my fellow human beings, not as an end in itself. I chose the entrepreneurial lifestyle because I enjoy the thrill of adventure, the challenge of growing a business.

2
I use my whole being.

I apply all my learnings and use all the skills I have. I draw knowledge from my reservoir of experience. Every day in business I experience a full mental workout.

3
I appreciate my independence.

I am the founder and leader of my entrepreneurial expedition. I am thankful to live in a country where I have the right to pursue my dreams. I am journeying down a path I have chosen. I am in control of my life.

4
I aim high.

I have confidence in my ability to grow a phenomenally successful company. I believe in my imagination and my ability. I have the courage to act on my ideas.

5
I am a cautious, alert traveler.

I take only calculated risks. I strive to lead a safe expedition, to safeguard my lifestyle and the lifestyle of those who accompany me. I make decisions with the knowledge that they have an impact on me, my suppliers, my employees, and all our families.

6
I have a firm vision.

I am journeying toward my North Star. However, I am a flexible traveler. I am open to changing my course to adapt to changes in the environment or to circumvent impediments in the terrain.

7
I take pleasure in the adventure.

I savor the smells, sights, and sounds in the jungle of entrepreneurship. I enjoy the process, the daily events that make my business unique. Every hour of my life brings new challenges and pleasures. I celebrate my achievements, both big and small. I love what I do every day.

8
I am part of a balanced ecosystem.

I recognize my ability and responsibility to improve the society in which I live. I respect the entrepreneurs with whom I do business as essential participants in the ecosystem. They thrive and I thrive. I take and I give. I understand that my actions influence many residents of the jungle, and their actions have an impact on my journey.

ACKNOWLEDGMENTS

The ideas, strategies, and reflections in this book are the outcomes of interactions with family members, associates, employees, suppliers, customers, competitors, journalists, seminar attendees, readers, and many others. I express my deepest gratitude to all who have helped shape my perspectives on business and life in general.

To David, my father and business partner, whose passion for living, appreciation of the aesthetic, love of philosophical challenges, unwavering positive attitude, regard for the elegance of written words, and belief in my abilities have cultivated my entrepreneurial spirit and inspired my creativity.

To Bianca, my mother and mentor, whose love of learning, intellectual insight, sensitive management techniques, displays of compassion, boundless energy, and esteem for art and culture have stimulated my imagination and enriched my soul.

To Sara, my sister and best friend, whose splendid sense of humor, steadfast determination, spontaneous funkiness, and constant curiosity continually spark the child within me.

To Gerda Levy, my grandmother and advisor, whose business wisdom has illuminated my path through the jungle of entrepreneurship.

To Marian Bernstein, my grandmother and fan, whose support and enthusiasm have encouraged me to continue striving.

To Richard Cohn and Cynthia Black, publishers and visionaries, who believed in me from the start, helped me champion a positive new activity for America's young people, and most recently, recognized the meaning of the adventure perspective.

To Joe Hammond, comrade in the creative process, whose imagination, appreciation for eloquent language, colloquial writing style, careful research, patience, flexibility, and inquisitiveness helped make this book what it is.

To Sue Mann, editor, who carefully, painstakingly, and meticulously transformed a raw manuscript into a polished, meaningful book.

To Jennifer Wong, executive assistant, who entered editorial corrections into the computer in the final stages of publication.

To Marvin Moore, proofreader, who fine-tuned the text and tied up loose ends.

To Bill Brunson, typographer, and the designers at Principia Graphica, who skillfully projected the spirit of adventure entrepreneurship onto the printed page.

To John Murphy, Barbara Barnes, and the other professionals at the Flinn Foundation, who gave me incentive to make the wonderful state of Arizona the launching point for my adventures.

To the entrepreneurs with whom I have conversed over the years and those interviewed specifically for this book, who have generously shared their trials and triumphs for the benefit of many others.

To all the stakeholders in my companies, employees, suppliers, customers, and others, who have embraced my visions for growth and improvement.

I feel fortunate to owe acknowledgment to so many admirable people. Lastly, I am forever thankful to live and work in the United States of America, where I am free to think, speak, write, and launch numerous expeditions into the jungle of entrepreneurship.

A B O U T A U T H O R S

Daryl Bernstein is a phenomenally successful entrepreneur and a leading speaker, writer, and consultant.

He has been featured on major television and radio networks on four continents, including CBS, CNN, National Public Radio, BBC, and Radio 3 Hong Kong. Articles about his books and businesses have appeared in hundreds of newspapers and magazines, including *The Wall Street Journal*, *The New York Times*, *The Dallas Morning News*, *The Miami Herald*, *Kiplinger's Personal Finance*, and *National Geographic World*.

Thousands have enjoyed the energy, humor, and insight of Bernstein's speeches, presentations, and seminars. He has enlighted and entertained audiences from Los Angeles to London. Twice he has been a featured guest speaker at Anthony Robbins's celebrated "Financial Mastery" seminar.

Through his consulting and training firm, Daryl Bernstein International, he is personal advisor and coach to entrepreneurs starting and growing small companies. (For information, fax 602-860-8650.)

Bernstein's original mission in writing was to motivate and educate young people. His first book, *Better Than a Lemonade Stand*, launched an international movement in youth entrepreneurship. Today he continues this effort by devoting a portion of his time to speak to children in schools across the United States.

The Geneva-based World Economic Forum named Bernstein a Global Leader for Tomorrow, one of a select few who "have already achieved great distinction in their leadership and are shaping our world beyond the year 2000."

Daryl Bernstein lives in Scottsdale, Arizona.

Joe Hammond applies his expertise in nineteenth-century literature to current social and economic issues. A professional researcher and writer, he lives in Ohio and Arizona.

NOTES

Chapter 1: The Adventure of Business

1. Helen Wright and Samuel Rapport, *The Great Explorers* (New York: Harper and Brothers, 1957), p. 438.

Chapter 2: The Spirit of Adventure Entrepreneurship

1. Louis E. Boone, *Quotable Business* (New York: Random House, 1992).
2. *Entrepreneur* magazine, June 1993, p. 77.
3. Richard Whittingham, *The Rand McNally Almanac of Adventure* (Chicago: Rand McNally, 1982), p. 43.
4. John G. Seamon and Douglas T. Kenrick, *Psychology* (Englewood Cliffs, N.J.: Prentice Hall, 1994), pp. 337–339.
5. *Entrepreneur*, February 1992, p. 68.
6. G. R. Crone, *The Explorers* (New York: Thomas Y. Crowell, 1962), p. 325.
7. *Entrepreneur*, June 1993, p. 90.
8. Crone, *Explorers*, p. 90.
9. Boone, *Quotable Business*, p. 239.

Chapter 3: Courage

1. Wright and Rapport, *Great Explorers*, p. 514.
2. Roger von Oech, *A Whack on the Side of the Head* (New York: Warner Books, 1983), p. 94.
3. Wright and Rapport, *Great Explorers*, p. 431.
4. *Entrepreneur*, August 1992, p. 60.
5. Maurice Sendak, *There's a Nightmare in My Closet* (New York: Dial Press, 1968).

Chapter 4: Optimism

1. Joseph R. Mancuso, *Mid-Career Entrepreneur* (Chicago: Dearborn Publishing, 1993), p. 33.
2. *Entrepreneur*, June 1992, p. 100.
3. Wright and Rapport, *Great Explorers*, p. 172.
4. David Livingstone, *Missionary Travels and Researches in South Africa* (1857; reprint, London: John Murray, 1912), p. 54.
5. Martin E. P. Seligman, *Learned Optimism* (New York: Alfred A. Knopf, 1990), p. 221.
6. Stephen R. Covey and A. Roger Merrill, *First Things First* (New York: Simon and Schuster, 1994).

Chapter 5: Flexibility

1. *Entrepreneur*, June 1993, p. 91.
2. Ibid., p. 72.
3. *Entrepreneur*, December 1992, p. 122.
4. Anthony Robbins, *Awaken the Giant Within* (New York: Summit Books, 1991), p. 278.

Chapter 6: Belief

1. Thomas J. Watson Jr. and Peter Petre, *Father, Son and Co.* (New York: Bantam Books, 1990), pp. 28–30.
2. Livingstone, *Missionary Travels*, p. 189.
3. Ibid., p. 10.
4. Mancuso, *Mid-Career Entrepreneur*, p. 21.
5. Robert E. Peary, *Nearest the Pole* (New York: Doubleday, Page, 1907), p. 18.
6. Meryle Gellman and Diane Gage, *The Confidence Quotient* (New York: World Almanac Publications, 1985), p. 86.
7. Ibid., p. 86.

Chapter 7: Decisiveness

1. Bruce Goodmansen, *It's a Jungle Out There* (Salt Lake City: Gibbs Smith, 1994), p. 78.

Chapter 8: Action

1. *Entrepreneur*, June 1992, p. 102.
2. Ibid., p. 113.
3. Wright and Rapport, *Great Explorers*, p. 81.

Chapter 9: Imagination

1. Wright and Rapport, *Great Explorers*, p. 25.
2. *Entrepreneur*, October 1992, p. 114.
3. Speech by Les Brown, The People's Network seminar, Scottsdale, Arizona, March 30, 1995.
4. *Newsweek*, February 19, 1990, pp. 52-53.

Introduction to Part III: The Adventure Principles

1. Wright and Rapport, *Great Explorers*, p. 539.

Chapter 10: Learn the Terrain Before You Embark

1. Wright and Rapport, *Great Explorers*, pp. 81-83.
2. Livingstone, *Missionary Travels*, p. 9.
3. Robbins, *Awaken Giant*, p. 496.
4. *Inc.*, January 1994, p. 29.
5. *Inc.*, September 1994, p. 67.
6. Peary, *Nearest Pole*, p. 80.
7. James Wallace and Jim Erickson, *Hard Drive* (New York: HarperBusiness, 1992), pp. 330-333.
8. A. David Silver, *Entrepreneurial Megabucks* (New York: John Wiley and Sons, 1985), pp. 370-371.

Chapter 11: Equip Yourself Well

1. Seamon and Kenrick, *Psychology*, pp. 337-339.
2. Wright and Rapport, *Great Explorers*, p. 179.
3. Livingstone, *Missionary Travels*, p. 34.
4. Crone, *Explorers*, p. 5.
5. *Success*, October 1994, p. 14.

Chapter 12: Aim for the Big Game

1. Speech by Les Brown, The People's Network seminar, Scottsdale, Arizona, March 30, 1995.
2. Michael Gerber, *The E Myth* (New York: HarperBusiness, 1986), pp. 58-65.
3. Ibid., p. 58.

Chapter 13: When You Encounter a Ravine, Build a Bridge

1. Peary, *Nearest Pole*, p. 78.
2. Crone, *Explorers*, p. 309.
3. Livingstone, *Missionary Travels*, p. 155.

Chapter 14: Watch and Listen for Signs of Change

1. *Entrepreneur*, October 1992, p. 110.
2. Livingstone, *Missionary Travels*, p. 115.
3. Wright and Rapport, *Great Explorers*, p. 145.

Chapter 15: Focus on Your Company, Not on Your Competitors

1. Livingstone, *Missionary Travels*, p. 92.
2. *Advertising Age*, March 21, 1994, p. 35.
3. Crone, *Explorers*, p. 122.
4. Ibid., p. 42.
5. Ibid., p. 122.
6. Livingstone, *Missionary Travels*, p. 110.

Chapter 16: Enjoy the Small Pleasures

1. Wright and Rapport, *Great Explorers*, p. 91.
2. Ibid., p. 432.
3. Crone, *Explorers*, p. 204.
4. Ibid., p. 32.
5. Whittingham, *Rand McNally*, p. 53.
6. Wright and Rapport, *Great Explorers*, p. 417.

Chapter 17: Calculate Every Risk

1. *Business Week/Enterprise*, 1993, pp. 104–105.
2. Ibid., p. 108.

Chapter 18: Consult Your Compass Frequently

1. Boone, *Quotable Business*, p. 7.
2. Desmond Wilcox, *Ten Who Dared* (Boston: Little, Brown, 1977), p. 11.
3. *Entrepreneur*, September 1992, p. 74.
4. Wright and Rapport, *Great Explorers*, pp. 91–92.

Chapter 19: Blaze Your Own Trail

1. *Newsweek*, February 19, 1990, pp. 52–53.
2. *Fortune*, January 30, 1989, p. 155, and July 25, 1994, p. 246.
3. *Business Week*, November 14, 1994, p. 44.
4. *World Link*, January/February 1993, pp. 80–85.

Chapter 20: Visioning

1. Lewis Carroll, *Alice's Adventures in Wonderland* (New York: Wanderer Books, 1982), p. 62.
2. *Entrepreneur*, October 1992, p. 124.
3. Stephen R. Covey, *The Seven Habits of Highly Effective People* (New York: Fireside, 1989), p. 98.
4. Livingstone, *Missionary Travels*, p. 111.
5. *Inc.*, September 1994, p. 76.
6. Wright and Rapport, *Great Explorers*, p. 93.

Chapter 21: Choosing a Business Adventure

1. Tom Peters, *The Pursuit of Wow!* (New York: Vintage Books, 1994), p. 22.
2. Mark McCormack, *What They Don't Teach You at Harvard Business School* (New York: Bantam Books, 1984), p. 161.
3. Robert Kriegl, *If It Ain't Broke . . . Break It!* (New York: Warner Books, 1991), pp. 258-259.
4. *Entrepreneur*, June 1993, p. 89.
5. Livingstone, *Missionary Travels*, p. 221.
6. *Entrepreneur*, October 1992, p. 116.

Chapter 22: Assembling Your Expeditionary Team

1. Whittingham, *Rand McNally*, pp. 211-212.
2. *Entrepreneur*, February 1992, p. 69.
3. Douchan Gersi, *Explorer* (Los Angeles: Jeremy P. Tarcher, 1987), p. 107.
4. *Entrepreneur*, October 1992, p. 116.
5. Joseph J. Fucini and Suzy Fucini, *Entrepreneurs* (Boston: G. K. Hall, 1985), p. 33.
6. *Inc.*, September 1994, p. 73.
7. Whittingham, *Rand McNally*, pp. 39-40.

Chapter 23: Interdependence in the Jungle

1. Paul Hawken, *The Ecology of Commerce* (New York: HarperCollins, 1993), p. xiii.
2. Wayne Dosick, *The Business Bible* (New York: William Morrow, 1993), p. 121.
3. *The Arizona Republic*, May 10, 1995, p. D1.
4. Livingstone, *Missionary Travels*, p. 74.
5. Dosick, *Business Bible*, p. 71.

Chapter 24: Growing a Business

1. *Nation's Business*, February 1992, p. 30.
2. *Entrepreneur*, June 1992, p. 107.
3. Peary, *Nearest Pole*, p. 35.
4. Wright and Rapport, *Great Explorers*, p. 177.
5. Crone, *Explorers*, p. 359.
6. Livingstone, *Missionary Travels*, p. 100.
7. Ibid., p. 102.

SUGGESTED READINGS

Collier, Lindsay. *Get Out of Your Thinking Box*. San Francisco: Robert D. Reed, 1994.

Covey, Stephen R. *The Seven Habits of Highly Effective People*. New York: Fireside, 1989.

·Covey, Stephen R. and A. Roger Merrill. *First Things First*. New York: Simon and Schuster, 1994.

Crone, G. R. *The Explorers*. New York: Thomas Y. Crowell, 1962.

Dosick, Wayne. *The Business Bible*. New York: William Morrow, 1993.

Emmerling, John. *It Only Takes One*. New York: Simon and Schuster, 1991.

Gellman, Meryle, and Diane Gage. *The Confidence Quotient*. New York: World Almanac Publications, 1985.

Gerber, Michael. *The E Myth*. New York: HarperBusiness, 1986.

Gersi, Douchan. *Explorer*. Los Angeles: Jeremy P. Tarcher, 1987.

Hawken, Paul. *The Ecology of Commerce*. New York: HarperCollins, 1993.

Kriegl, Robert. *If It Ain't Broke . . . Break It!* New York: Warner Books, 1991.

Levinson, Jay Conrad. *Guerrilla Marketing*. New York: Houghton Mifflin, 1993.

Livingstone, David. *Missionary Travels and Researches in South Africa*. 1857. Reprint, Salem, N.H.: Ayer, 1972.

Mancuso, Joseph R. *Mid-Career Entrepreneur*. Chicago: Dearborn Publishing, 1993.

McCormack, Mark. *What They Don't Teach You at Harvard Business School*. New York: Bantam Books, 1984.

Peary, Robert E. *Nearest the Pole*. New York: Doubleday, Page, 1907.

Peters, Tom. *The Pursuit of Wow!* New York: Vintage Books, 1994.

Robbins, Anthony. *Awaken the Giant Within*. New York: Summit Books, 1991.

Seligman, Martin E. P. *Learned Optimism*. New York: Alfred A. Knopf, 1990.

Silver, A. David. *Entrepreneurial Megabucks*. New York: John Wiley and Sons, 1985.

Von Oech, Roger. *A Whack on the Side of the Head*. New York: Warner Books, 1983.

Wallace, James, and Jim Erickson. *Hard Drive*. New York: Harper-Business, 1992.

Watson, Thomas J., Jr., and Peter Petre. *Father, Son and Co*. New York: Bantam Books, 1990.

Wilcox, Desmond. *Ten Who Dared*. Boston: Little, Brown, 1977.

Wright, Helen, and Samuel Rapport. *The Great Explorers*. New York: Harper and Brothers, 1957.

Hindsights:
The Wisdom and Breakthroughs of Remarkable People
Author: Guy Kawasaki, $22.95 hardcover

What have you learned from your life that you would like to share with the next generation? Get a fresh appreciation of the human experience in this inspirational collection of interviews with thirty-three people who have overcome unique challenges. They are candid about their failures and disappointments, and insightful about turning adversity into opportunity. Guy Kawasaki spent over two years researching and interviewing such people as Apple Computer co-founder Steve Wozniak, management guru Tom Peters, and entrepreneur May Kay. But not everyone in the book is a celebrity. They share their revelations and life experiences, motivating the reader for both personal and professional growth.

When Money Is Not Enough: Fulfillment in Work
Author: Eileen R. Hannegan, M.S., $10.95 softcover

In an age when Americans spend more than half their waking hours either at work or performing a function related to work, it is important that the workplace be a healthy community rather than a chaotic battleground. *When Money Is Not Enough* offers the premise that when personality battles create stress and illness, no amount of money in the world is enough to justify continued employment. The book is neither pro-employer nor pro-employee in its approach. Instead, it encourages increasing interdependence among all staff members. Approaching the workplace as a community or family is the key to resolving problems. Drawing from her years of experience as a consultant and lecturer in family systems and organizational development, author Eileen R. Hannegan offers proven methods of transforming the workplace from toxic to healthy. Work can indeed enhance life as well as pay the bills.

The Woman's Book of Creativity

Author: C Diane Ealy, $12.95 softcover

Creativity works differently in women and men, and women are most creative when they tap into the process that is unique to their own nature—a holistic, "spiraling" approach. The book is a self-help manual, both inspirational and practical, for igniting female creative fire. Ealy encourages women to acknowledge their own creativity, often in achievements they take for granted. She also gives a wealth of suggestions and exercises to enable women to recognize their own creative power and to access it consistently and effectively. Ealy holds a doctorate in behavioral science and consults with individuals and corporations on creativity.

Seeing Without Glasses: Improving Your Vision Naturally

Author: Dr. Robert-Michael Kaplan, $12.95 softcover; $19.95 hardcover

Seeing Without Glasses invites you to become an active participant in maintaining vision-fitness and preventing eye problems. The premise is stunningly simple: Eye fitness can be developed in exactly the same way other parts of the body are toned—through exercise and diet. Businesses benefit as productivity increases when their employees use preventive techniques to avoid computer eyestrain and to reduce the negative side effects of vision stress. This is a valuable handbook for anyone looking to improve his or her vision or to maintain healthy eyesight.

Know Your Truth, Speak Your Truth, Live Your Truth
Author: Eileen R. Hannegan, $12.95 softcover

To be truly yourself, you need to have an authentic integration of the mental, emotional, physical, and spiritual truths of self. This book offers a simplified formula of the ancient truths that escort an individual into personal and spiritual wholeness. The three-part program assists individuals in discovering the truth of who they truly are and thereby in living a more authentic life.

You Can Have It All
Author: Arnold M. Patent, $16.95 hardcover

Joy, peace, abundance—these gifts of the Universe are available to each of us whenever we choose to play the real game of life: the game of mutual support. *You Can Have It All* is a guidebook that shows us how to move beyond our beliefs in struggle and shortage, open our hearts, and enjoy a life of true ecstasy. Arnold Patent first self-published *You Can Have It All* in 1984, and it became a classic with over 200,000 copies in print. This revised and expanded edition reflects his greater understanding of the principles and offers practical suggestions as well as simple exercises for improving the quality of our lives.

To order or to request a catalog, contact
Beyond Words Publishing, Inc.
4443 NE Airport Road
Hillsboro, OR 97124-6074
503-693-8700 or 1-800-284-9673

Beyond Words Publishing, Inc.

Our corporate mission:

Inspire to Integrity

Our declared values:

We give to all of life as life has given us.

We honor all relationships.

Trust and stewardship are integral to fulfilling dreams.

Collaboration is essential to create miracles.

Creativity and aesthetics nourish the soul.

Unlimited thinking is fundamental.

Living your passion is vital.

Joy and humor open our hearts to growth.

It is important to remind ourselves of love.